'Michael Robbins develops a new way of looking at language and its dual psychological and sociological roles, one that emerges from his extensive clinical experience. The new proposals that he offers are interesting, exciting and novel. I know that I will come back to his work multiple times to contemplate these original proposals on language, consciousness, mental health, and psychological development. A welcome addition to the literature on human language and psychology.'

—**Daniel L. Everett**, Dean of Arts and Sciences at Bentley University; formerly Chair of the Department of Languages, Literatures and Cultures at Illinois State University; author of *Don't Sleep, There are Snakes.*

'This is a book of striking originality and of great significance for psychoanalysts, psychiatrists, psychologists but also for all those who have sought to understand and articulate the way in which human beings communicate between themselves. Novelists, writers and those who lecture and speech makers will profit enormously from reading this book and absorbing deeply its message. Michael Robbins brings to light that there are two forms of communication between persons: representational language and primordial consciousness. To illustrate these two forms of communication I will take an example from my own experience. In London in the 70s I had an analysis five times a week with a little-known psychoanalyst. When I first approached him I was severely ill mentally. When the analysis was over I was a changed person. I was fit and well. That this came about through the analysis I have no doubt. But, what was it that my analyst communicated that had such a healing power? It was not his interpretations, that which he articulated in representational language but an inner spirit of generosity and wisdom which was not articulated in representational language but was infused in primordial consciousness. I had known this for some years but not until reading Michael Robbins' book was I able to voice it in a form that made complete sense of my own experience but also held immediate conviction for me that this form of communication had an importance in daily social life that was relevant for writers, for literary critics, for speech makers and all who are concerned with how human messaging occurs in any culture or community.'

—**Neville Symington**, author, former President of the Australian Psychoanalytic Society, and recipient of the Sigourney award of the International Psychoanalytic Association.

'Michael Robbins goes yet more deeply into his exploration of early mentation, which he first revealed to us in *Experiences of Schizophrenia and The Primordial Mind in Health and Illness*. In *Consciousness, Language, and Self* he explores the hidden meaning of language in its normal and pathological forms. Neurophysiology, psychoanalysis, infant research, relational theories and clinical experience are masterfully interwoven to form an intellectual tour de force that sheds new light on the exploration of the mental processes at the root of the sense of self. His patients' essays offer unique empirical access to the mind's most intimate and mysterious elements. Robbins' creative yet rigorous study of language will guide the reader into the innermost part of the human mind. This book is essential reading for every analyst interested in primitive mental states and psychosis, all clinicians, practitioners and students of mental health will be enlightened by this vibrant and profound contribution.'

—**Riccardo Lombardi**, author of *Formless Infinity, Clinical Explorations of Matte Blanco and Bion* and *Body–Mind Dissociation*

Consciousness, Language, and Self

Consciousness, Language, and Self proposes that the human self is innately bilingual. Conscious mind includes two qualitatively distinct mental processes, each of which uses the same formal elements of language differently. The "mother tongue," the language of primordial consciousness, begins *in utero* and our second language, reflective symbolic thought, begins in infancy.

Michael Robbins describes the respective roles the two conscious mental processes and their particular use of language play in the course of normal and pathological development, as well as the role the language of primordial consciousness plays in adult life in such phenomena as dreaming, infant-caregiver attachment, creativity, belief systems and their effects on social and political life, cultural differences, and psychosis. Examples include creative persons, extreme political figures and psychotic individuals. Five original essays, written by the author's current and former patients, describe what they learned about their aberrant uses of language and their origins.

This book sheds new light on several controversies that have been limited by the incorrect assumption that reflective representational thought and its language is the only conscious mental state. These include the debate within linguistics about whether language is the expression of a hardwired instinct whose identifying feature is recursion; within psychoanalysis about the nature of conscious and unconscious mental processes, and within cognitive philosophy about whether language and thought are isomorphic.

Consciousness, Language, and Self will be of great value to psychoanalysts, as well as students and scholars of linguistics, cognitive philosophy and cultural anthropology.

Michael Robbins is a psychoanalyst and was formerly professor of clinical psychiatry at Harvard Medical School and the University of California San Francisco. He is a member of the American and International Psychoanalytic Associations. His previous books include *Experiences of Schizophrenia*, *Conceiving of Personality*, and *The Primordial Mind in Health and Illness: A Cross-Cultural Perspective*.

Consciousness, Language, and Self

Psychoanalytic, Linguistic, and
Anthropological Explorations of
the Dual Nature of Mind

Michael Robbins

LONDON AND NEW YORK

First published 2018
by Routledge
2 Park Square, Milton Park, Abingdon, Oxon OX14 4RN

and by Routledge
711 Third Avenue, New York, NY 10017

Routledge is an imprint of the Taylor & Francis Group, an informa business

© 2018 Michael Robbins

The right of Michael Robbins to be identified as author of this work has been asserted by him in accordance with sections 77 and 78 of the Copyright, Designs and Patents Act 1988.

All rights reserved. No part of this book may be reprinted or reproduced or utilised in any form or by any electronic, mechanical, or other means, now known or hereafter invented, including photocopying and recording, or in any information storage or retrieval system, without permission in writing from the publishers.

Trademark notice: Product or corporate names may be trademarks or registered trademarks, and are used only for identification and explanation without intent to infringe.

British Library Cataloguing in Publication Data
A catalogue record for this book is available from the British Library

Library of Congress Cataloging in Publication Data
A catalog record for this book has been requested

ISBN: 978-1-138-48763-5 (hbk)
ISBN: 978-1-138-48764-2 (pbk)
ISBN: 978-1-351-03962-8 (ebk)

Typeset in Times New Roman and Gill Sans
by Florence Production Ltd, Stoodleigh, Devon, UK

Contents

Acknowledgements vii
Preface ix

Introduction: The lay of the land 1

1 Language and the sense of self 5

2 Two conscious mental processes and their languages 11

3 Theoretical background of the problem of mental process and consciousness 15

4 Fundamental manifestations of primordial consciousness: dreaming and the languages of mother-infant bonding 25

5 The relation of mental process and language: the controversy within linguistics 29

6 The relationship of language to thought and the sense of self 33

7 Belief systems and other everyday phenomenology of primordial consciousness and its language 37

8 Primordial consciousness, language, and cultural differences 47

9 Emergence of the bilingual sense of self during the attachment phase 53

10 What characterizes language aberration? 61

11 Language aberration in relation to pathology of early
     attachment   69

12 Clinical methodology and data   77

Patient essays

13 Caroline: Schizophrenese   83

14 Jane   101

15 Charles   111

16 Lisabeth   119

17 Jacob   135

18 Our languages and our selves: discussion and conclusion   149

    References   155
    Index   163

Acknowledgements

An author of a book aspires to teach. In order to be a teacher one must have something to teach, therefore one must first and foremost be a student and learner. The kind of learning to which I refer cannot be accomplished by sitting in an ordinary classroom. It requires personal experience.

My intellectual odyssey that eventuated in the ideas I present in the pages to come is outlined in the Preface. Much of what informs the book has been learned from sitting in a different kind of classroom: one taught by my patients, on the subject of how mind works. While they must remain anonymous for reasons of confidentiality I want to express gratitude to the current and former patients who have shared what they learned about themselves and their language in the five essays that illustrate the book.

I would like to thank Mark Poster, MD, for reading the first iteration of the book, in its early incarnation as a paper that soon outgrew acceptable page limits. I am especially grateful to Arnold Wyse, MD, and Myrna Wyse, MSW, for their careful reading and critical comments.

Most of all I want to express gratitude to Karen Sheingold, Ph.D, who read the book in parts and in its entirely more than once, and whose continuing constructive dissatisfaction motivated me to rethink, clarify and improve what I was trying to say.

Preface

I have always loved language, and over the years I have been intrigued and curious about my patients' linguistic idiosyncrasies. The inspiration for the book came from my realization that many of these are reflections of a manifestation of conscious mind qualitatively different from ordinary thought. The scope of my investigation gradually expanded to encompass language as a reflection and expression of mind as a whole, not just what is idiosyncratic or pathological. Eventually I reached the conclusion that humans are intrinsically bilingual. We "speak" two languages; a "mother tongue," and a second language, but the distinction between the two is obscured by the fact that each uses the same formal vocabulary and sentence structure. Along with this realization came the awareness that many of the seemingly separate subjects I have written about over the course of my professional career, beginning with my very first (1969) publication, on artistic creativity in *The Psychoanalytic Study of the Child*, can be integrated to support this hypothesis. These subjects include, in addition to creativity, the psychoses, dreaming, the dual nature of conscious mind, linguistics, cultural differences, and the nature of personality and the sense of self. In 1993 I wrote a book on schizophrenia, the most severe of the psychoses, and the peculiarities of language and sense of self that characterize it, an interest I pursued further in a 2002 paper on language and delusion in schizophrenia and in my third book in 2011. In 1996 I explored the concept of self in a book called *Conceiving of Personality*. My interest in dreaming and the mental activity that produces it led to papers in 2004 and 2015. In a 2008 paper, in my 2011 book on the primordial mind, and in another paper, that should be in print in the journal *Psychoanalytic Inquiry* at the same time as this book, I focus on Freud's primary process and its relation to the complex and confusing subject of the nature of conscious and unconscious mind. In a 2002 paper I ventured into linguistics and in the 2011 book, cultural differences and their implications for psychoanalytic theory. In my 2011 book *The Primordial Mind in Health and Illness* I began the process of integrating these subjects under the hypothesis of two qualitatively different forms of mental activity, a process that I continue and elaborate in the pages to come. At the time I believed one of these processes was unconscious; I have come to believe that both are conscious, and play a major role in our everyday lives.

Introduction
The lay of the land

The impetus to write the book arose out of my intrigue and curiosity about the unusual mental processes and related idiosyncratic uses of language of some of my patients whose problems fall at various points on the psychotic spectrum. But it has turned into a book that is broader in scope; more about language and its vicissitudes than about psychosis, which reflects but one unusual and pathological use of language. As I developed my ideas the scope of the book broadened to encompass the early development of the sense of self and the concurrent emergence of language, interior and external, as an expression of it.

I came to the conclusion that we are all bilingual; not in the sense of the superficial morphological and grammatical characteristics of our native tongue that depends upon our geographical location and country of origin, but in a more fundamental sense. My hypothesis is that there are two qualitatively different forms of conscious mental activity, each of which uses language in a different way. The differences are not immediately apparent insofar as both utilize the same formal vocabulary and grammar. The defining characteristics of each of these are elaborated in chapter 2. The first of these, which I call primordial consciousness, is our "mother tongue" that begins *in utero*. Most of us develop a "second language" out of the matrix of mother-infant attachment and neural maturation, which I call reflective representational thought. However, the language of primordial consciousness remains selectively active throughout the course of our lives.

In chapter 3 I describe how the bilingual model is derived from the neuropsychological contributions of Julian Jaynes and the psychoanalytic contributions of Freud on consciousness, unconsciousness and the primary process, and its elaboration in other conceptual terms by Melanie Klein. The contributions of Jaynes to mind are distinguished from his neurological speculations and their strengths and limitations are examined. Freud's model, however, suffers from inconsistency, contradiction and confusion as he believed the mental activity he named the primary process to be qualitatively different from conscious thought. He thought of it as unconscious in the sense of being invisible to conscious mind. However, in a seeming contradiction, he described its visible conscious characteristics. Hence he believed that there is but one form of consciousness and language with which to express it. Freud was unable to fully appreciate the most truly revolutionary aspects of his discovery and hence relegated to a mysterious invisible realm known as the unconscious the mental activity I call primordial consciousness and the language with which it is expressed.

In chapter 4 I describe the two fundamental phenomena reflective of primordial consciousness and its language: dreaming, and motherese, the language of mother-infant bonding.

The bilingual model of mind illuminates problems in contemporary linguistic and psychoanalytic theories and the cognitive philosophy of thought, as well as helping to elucidate the foundation of many phenomena of everyday life, normal and pathological. These problems have arisen from the equation of consciousness, dating from Descartes, with reflection and introspection, so that it is commonly believed that there is but a single manifestation of consciousness, reflective representational thought, and a single fundamental language with which to express it.

In chapter 5 I examine the controversy within the field of linguistics about the essential or defining characteristics of language and the relative contributions of biology and environment to its development. The dominant viewpoint within linguistics known by various names including universal grammar is that language is basically hardwired or instinctual in origin and there is but a single language template, based on the principle of recursion. This belief has been challenged by environmentalists, a few of whom believe that recursion is not an essential feature of language, but the debate has been limited to "is it or isn't it?" I conclude that this conceptual myopia is based on the incorrect assumption that equates language with reflective representational thought and hence defines it as recursive in nature. The model I propose, of two qualitatively different forms of consciousness each of which uses language differently, clarifies that the language of reflective representational thought conforms to the principle of recursion but the language of primordial consciousness does not. This concept shifts the debate from one all-encompassing model of language whose origin is genetic, to more complex questions about languages – our mother tongue and second language – and the respective roles of heredity and environment in their development.

Chapter 6 examines the relationship of language to thought, and to one's sense of self.

Chapters 7 and 8 describe how the model of primordial consciousness and reflective representational thought, their respective linguistic expressions and the interaction between them, enables a new understanding of other phenomena both normal and pathological, including psychosis, differences between individual-centric and socio-centric cultures, creativity, dogmatic belief systems that lead to radical movements, religions, and extreme political events.

In the realms of sociology and politics belief systems that captivate groups of people and their widely varied social consequences comprise one of the most striking manifestations of primordial consciousness. Using as illustration the problem of destructive political upheaval in the world at the time of writing the book, chapters 7, 10 and 11 contrast two contemporary cultural icons each of whose belief systems reflects primordial consciousness and its language yet whose ways of trying to bring about change represent the fundamentally opposite poles of war and peace. Bob Dylan was awarded the 2016 Nobel Prize in Literature, and Donald Trump is in the early stages of his presidency of the United States as I write this book.

Chapters 9 and 11 are devoted to the process of self-formation and the interdependent emergence of the two forms of consciousness, and their respective languages and the sense of self they create during the early attachment phase. The language of primordial consciousness, that commences during the last trimester of intrauterine life, is our "mother tongue," whereas reflective representational thought, which develops later, utilizes what is, in a sense, a second language. In the course of maturation each plays an important role, and the nature of the ultimate relationship between the two is unique to each individual and each culture.

When the process of attachment and the development of a bilingual self goes awry, adult language may become aberrant, a subject I elaborate in chapters 10 and 11. Language aberration is the product of a combination of factors: primordial consciousness, which of itself is neither normal nor abnormal, and distortions of the sense of self and world derived from pathology of the attachment phase in the context of which it develops. The continued use of primordial consciousness and its language beyond the time when reflective representational thought is contextually appropriate and should predominate in ordinary social situations, enables the child to avoid experiencing the threat of separation from the primary undifferentiated relationship with the mothering person. There is an important distinction between language aberrations and their origins, and their manifestations which may or may not be labelled pathological, depending on their interpersonal and social consequences.

I have been fortunate to work with a group of former and current patients who in the course of intensive psychoanalytic therapy became interested in, knowledgeable and even articulate about their own linguistic idiosyncrasies and their origins in disturbed early attachment patterns. Five of them kindly agreed to write about this and their amazing essays provide firsthand insight into the nature of normal, aberrant, and pathological development of language and the emergent sense of self. After a discussion of methodology and use of this kind of data in chapter 12, I present those essays, along with my commentary, in chapters 13 through 17, followed by chapter 18, the conclusion.

Chapter 1

Language and the sense of self

Robert Burns's 1786 poem *To a Louse: On Seeing One on a Lady's Bonnet at Church* highlights the contrast between how we are viewed by others within our social and cultural context, based on a variety of evidence we give off, behavioral and verbal, advertent and inadvertent, and our very own internal sense of self, which is largely reflected in our language. As Burns humorously depicts, the two may be quite discrepant. In a non-dialectical English translation it goes like this:

> And would some Power the gift give us
> to see ourselves as others see us!
> It would from many a blunder free us,
> And foolish notion:
> What airs in dress and gait would leave us,
> And even devotion!

Language, as well as expression and gesture, is the way we present ourselves to the world, and along with aspects of mind that might be not be verbalized, is the way we know ourselves. The book presents the hypothesis that humans are essentially bilingual. The formal aspects of language – vocabulary, grammar, syntax, morphology – are used in the service of semantics to express meaning that reflects two qualitatively different conscious mental processes. For example, two formally identical statements may have totally different meanings depending on which mental process they are expressing.

By definition psychoanalysts are unusually interested in language. But perhaps I have been more so than many because of my particular interest in schizophrenia, a condition in which the language peculiarities with which the person frames his or her sense of self and the world are so strange that they are impossible to rationalize and hence to ignore. I have always been intrigued by some of the strange ideas of my patients and some of the equally strange ways they have of formulating them. For much of my career I more or less contented myself believing what I was taught in my psychoanalytic training that such things are symptoms; arcane symbols whose meaning is repressed and unconscious and whose meaning is to be explored indirectly through a process of free association and analysis of resistances that will eventually uncover the unconscious conflict that explains it all and in so doing reveal the underlying truth.

In time I realized that the central problem in psychosis is the failure of two processes essential to the creation of meaning: integration and differentiation. Some call the absence of integration fragmentation, others splitting or dissociation. The result of failure of differentiation is that in a psychological-meaning and not a formal cognitive sense the person cannot distinguish what is going on in his or her head from what is happening in the "real" outside world. The result of lack of integration is that contrary or contradictory ideas coexist in consciousness, hence the absence of conflict where in a mature mind one might expect it to be. And I realized that perhaps the unusual meanings were not so disguised and hidden as I had supposed but were plain to be seen if one grasped the idea that they were being expressed through a different mental operation and its unique use of language. In other words, the fact that the patient could not reflect upon his or her mental process in a mature way did not necessarily mean that the meanings were unconscious. Or to say it differently, the fact that the meanings were unconscious to reflective thought did not necessarily mean that they were not part of the person's conscious mental experience and process.

My interest expanded to dreaming, an activity whose underlying primary mental process Freud believed to be the basis of schizophrenia as well, and not without confusion and ambiguity believed it to be the essence of unconscious mind and to contain the symbols of unconscious conflict. I began to question the belief that dreaming is an unconscious process and to formulate the concept of two different conscious mental processes and their respective uses of language in a series of papers that came to fruition in my 2011 book. Since then I have become increasingly aware that we only know about the strange ideas through the strange but quite conscious language usage with which they are expressed. I further came to realize that the strangeness may not be at all apparent to the listener as the two mental processes use the same formal vocabulary and sentence structure.

Some of the most unusual uses of language are on the surface so unremarkable as not to attract notice. For example, the use of pronouns does not mean the same thing in the language of primordial consciousness as it does in the language of reflective representational thought. Listening from the perspective of reflective representational thought which supports introspection and the assessment by one aspect of the self of other aspects, the first person pronoun "I" implies self-awareness or self-consciousness. However, in the language of primordial consciousness "I" only implies agency or activity; doing or a sense of being. From a similar perspective one assumes the use of second or third person pronouns refers to a differentiated separate person, but in the undifferentiated language of primordial consciousness it denotes part of the speaker's intrapsychic self of which he or she is unaware and that is therefore believed to exist in the other person. Jacob (chapter 17) repeatedly said "you know," "you believe," "I think you are angry," or "you think that ...," when as best as I was aware I had no such thought or feeling, and in the case of "you know" the information was often something I had never heard before. He believed for a long time that our minds were one, and was unaware of some of his own mental content. He often assumed that he did not have to tell me many of his thoughts because I already knew them. These distinctions are not obvious as persons "speaking" in the language of primordial consciousness believe they are introspecting and reflecting as much as anyone else, and because they are coming from a position of belief, they can be quite convincing.

Moving to more arresting specimens of language, Caroline (chapter 13) became enraged when an acquaintance, in what sounded to me like a conventional expression of farewell kindness, said "take care." I eventually learned that Caroline heard not a good wish, but a concrete performative undifferentiated taking over of her mind compelling her to take responsibility for caring for herself; something that she was unable to conceptualize a right to differ with because she did not have a sense of herself as a separate person, and moreover, an idea that at core was so repugnant it enraged her. One of Caroline's oft repeated phrases in the early years of our work was "nothing good will ever happen." For a long time I took this as an ordinary language statement of depression and pessimism based on assessment of her unsatisfying life. Eventually I learned about her underlying rage, that she had never been able to formulate and represent as an emotion, and realized that she was making a concrete performative assertion of determination to destroy anything positive. Caroline would spend hours in scathing attacks on various people for not taking care of her according to her fantastic expectations. I came to realize that her reproach of others was an undifferentiated expression of a self-reproach for not caring about herself that she could not bear to acknowledge. Similarly her equally passionate admiration of other people for their maturity and responsibility represented an unintegrated part of her mind advocating responsibility that she angrily repudiated. She regularly wrote long "letters" to people she had little relationship to but was not able to differentiate from herself, often former caregivers, pouring out intimate details most people would feel ashamed to reveal. And we eventually realized that these reflected the belief she was actually evacuating aspects of herself she did not want to be responsible for.

Jane (chapter 14) got very agitated in the early stages of her treatment when (in the days I still wore them) I adjusted my tie. Her language reflected the literal belief I was masturbating. She, too, believed she could "tell" what I was thinking and feeling, sometimes from changes in my expression, many times from no obvious cues whatsoever. Although her professional writings showed unusual knowledge of such subjects, in her personal discourse she had almost no words for emotions or for body parts below her waist, and when she said "that's just words," she meant language had no bodily and emotional correlates. Her language permitted of the most fundamental contradictions so that at one point she seriously believed that if she shot herself in the head a flower garden would grow there.

Jacob (chapter 17), a man with a large formal vocabulary, had intense anxiety and verbal aphasia when it came to finding words to describe his inner life. When he was not busy attacking me he was paralyzed with uses of "maybe" and "I don't know." He "thought" in fragmentary pictorial images of body parts not linked to sequences of thought, accompanied by physical sensations and impulses.

He pictured me "sitting in shit" or began a session saying he felt like he had a knife in his pocket rather than being able to tell me he was angry. At times he said he felt that he had a breast, and he tried to brush it off. At other times he literally perceived me as a monster. These images reflected enactments of what we eventually identified as hatred he could neither integrate nor express in thoughtful language. Even when we had made some progress he would say "I'm making you into my mother;" not "You remind me of my mother." Instead of talking about his sense of worthlessness he would say "I feel like a brown Jewish boy" or he would be convinced he had a fatal disease. As shorthand I came to say to him at these times "Please try to speak English" (tell me about your anger, etc.) and he would often say "I don't like to know that . . .", or "I don't want to feel . . .", rather than "I'm unhappy at being this way." For many years we puzzled fruitlessly about a delusion that had ruined his early career in mathematics, namely the belief he could divide by zero, only to find ultimately that it concretely expressed his belief he needed to destroy everything important to him.

Charles's language aberration (chapter 15) was not so blatant. He lived in a world of body sensations and images, some of which he came to describe to me, but he had no words for emotions. In lieu of knowing about his anger he experienced somatic constrictions in gut and chest, and he had the undifferentiated conviction that my attentions to him were critical attacks. When I encouraged him to express his feelings so we would know what they were, rather than withhold, he concretely interpreted "express" to mean that I was encouraging him to attack me, rather than to articulate integrated thoughts of his own as a separate person that we might discuss.

Lisabeth (chapter 16) experienced her mind in words of physical imagery. During an early separation from me she literally felt her arms had been amputated. She could not tolerate separations because she could not differentiate herself from me. I no longer existed as a separate person she cared about and missed and she no longer existed, either. Rather, she experienced a sense of catastrophe associated with the feeling her arms had been amputated, and would make comments such as "I know you never think about me over the weekend." What she required was the belief that I was totally preoccupied with her existence so that I had no independent life whatsoever and we were not separate people. The notion of ending our relationship eventually, "terminating," as I unfortunately put it in one discussion, was not only not a goal of hers, but mention of the very word threw her into a concrete physical-affective state of panic, terror and nothingness, as she interpreted it literally as execution and the end of her existence. I eventually dubbed the state "the trap door is opening," in an effort to help her learn to reflect and use words to talk about it. Her self-esteem was abysmally low, and it was somatized and nonverbal. For a long time before she could conceptualize it as an emotional mental state all she could do was to tell me that she had diarrhea in the waiting room prior to our sessions. It was difficult to make any interpretive comment to her as the rage of which she was unaware was experienced in an undifferentiated way as me criticizing her and saying she was no good. As we began to make progress looking at some of her idiosyncratic language meanings she once told me "Don't confuse me with facts."

Our sense of self, "who you think you are," is largely based on language – both our inner speech and the words, the linguistic structures that frame them, and the tone or prosody with which we articulate them. No less an authority on the importance of language and the unfolding relationship of language and self than the Judeo-Christian biblical account of Genesis proclaims, "In the beginning was the word, and the word was with God, and the word was God" (King James version). Ludwig Wittgenstein said "The limits of my language means the limits of my world" (1922, p. 356). Rizzuto makes the interesting assertion "I call the result of this process [therapy] *the emotional history of words*. The history of the individual with his or her objects, as the result of such a process, is so clearly written in the language used by that individual that I could paraphrase Freud (1905) by saying that no one who speaks can keep secret major portions of his or her life history from the ears of a good listener" (2003, p. 292).

As I use the term in the discussion to follow, language is Janus faced. It comprises the social or socialized face of mind as well as the private inner vehicle by which we come to know ourselves and our thoughts and become our own companions as we grow to be separate individuals. It is the music, harmonious or strident, with which we harangue or solace ourselves when alone. Language is also the primary vehicle with which we express ourselves within the interpersonal and social contexts in which we live. When given voice it is communicative. The communicative function of language, however, does not necessarily express intention that the other can understand. Although it may consist of intentional sharing with other selves, it may express motivation not to share and be understood, or it may simply be a concrete vehicle of discharge in and onto a world of objects. To make things more complicated, if the speaker is unable to differentiate self from other, whatever his or her conscious intent and whatever language he or she uses, the result may yet be solipsistic rather than truly communicative to a separately perceived other.

While it is evident that people from different countries and different parts of the world speak different languages, what is not so apparent is that there is a deeper language difference at the core of each of us, regardless of country of origin or residence. We each, and in varying individual proportions, "speak" two languages: a "mother tongue" that I call primordial consciousness, and a later developing "second language" of reflective representational thought. As a consequence of the vicissitudes of early attachment and individual variations in use of the two languages of primordial consciousness and reflective representational thought, each person's resultant melding of language and its uses is unique. The sense of self associated with the mother tongue of primordial consciousness develops out of the undifferentiated matrix of the earliest efforts mothers and their infants make to attach to one another, affected by the innate mental equipment and motivation of the infant and the attunement and involvement or lack thereof that the primary caregiver provides in response. At the same time that language is the primary means by which we communicate with others as adults it is also the way we simultaneously psychologically reconnect with the primary other with whom our sense of self first developed, in whatever form, normal or pathological, that original attachment may have taken. As Freud so aptly put it, "the finding of an object is in fact a re-finding of it" (1905d, p. 222).

Though analyst and patient may speak the same language – English, Mandarin, whatever – in a formal sense, including grammar and syntax, and words that may naively be assumed to have shared meaning, what is communicated may not be what either party consciously intends or believes. Underlying what may seem on the surface like congruence in language-based understanding may be a deeper unexamined incongruence based on assumptions of the respective parties that they are communicating in what each believes to be reflective representational thought when in fact they may not be. The analytic encounter, focused as it is on language and on the transference, provides a unique opportunity to study what goes on beneath the formal language surface and to separate out the elements of bilingual self that are unique to each encounter.

In the pages to come I examine the origins of our bilingual sense of self in the context of the thesis that there are two qualitatively different mental processes: primordial consciousness and reflective representational thought. Each of these processes uses language in a fundamentally different way. In order to accomplish this task I critically review findings from psychoanalysis related to the primary process and consciousness; findings related to the attachment phase of early development and its role in language development and the formation of a sense of self, the controversy in linguistics between nature and nurture in the formation of language, and the relationship between language and thought. I present data provided by patients in long-term treatment who have gained awareness and insight into their own unusual uses of language and idiosyncratic senses of self to illustrate how, as a consequence of disruption and distortion of basic attachment during the earliest phase of self-formation the sense of self may become delusional. In such instances the language of primordial consciousness based on the original fusion of self and other persists, and the language of reflective representational thought which is realistically adaptive to a world in which self and other are separate beings, fails to develop.

Chapter 2
Two conscious mental processes and their languages

Language is an expression and reflection of mental activity. In my 2011 book *The Primordial Mind in Health and Illness* I described two qualitatively distinctive mental processes that play a major role in everyday human life. The mental process and its language that we in Western or individual-centric cultures generally think of when we think of conscious mind is reflective, representational, symbolic thought. Freud called it the secondary process. This is the mental process that develops during our early years of socialization as I describe in chapters 9 and 11. It is, in essence, a second language that arises along with the mental capacity to experience oneself as a separate individual rather than an undifferentiated part of the primordial soup. The thoughtful mind is capable of self-awareness and self-scrutiny as well as constant mental representations that can be abstracted and used symbolically because they are differentiated from the surrounding world and are not concrete and stimulus bound. The mind of reflective awareness can identify specific emotions and not be reflexively driven by their affective and somatic precursors. It is capable of differentiating what is going on within the bounds of a conceptualized self, the intrapsychic world, from what is going on in the external world, and therefore of appreciating a reality outside and independent of the self. It is capable of distinguishing aspects of mind that need to be contemplated and controlled from those one may choose to enact.

Most important, the thoughtful mind is Cartesian. It is capable of introspection, or what linguists call recursion. That is, "cogito, ergo sum." The mind can reflect or think about itself; it can be an object of its own inquiry and not just a subject that exists and acts totally in the moment. The thoughtful person is introspecting, remembering, appreciating the passage of time, questioning, and considering multiple perspectives rather than being concretely bound to an immediate stimulus and committed to a single belief or truth and the reflexively driven actions that would follow from it. The thoughtful mind is reasonable; more or less logical and rational.

When I wrote about the other mental process in 2011, I called it primordial mental activity and believed, along with Freud and others, that it is unconscious. I have come to think otherwise, and therefore have renamed it *primordial consciousness*. This conscious mental activity is immediate and stimulus-bound and hence is not recursive or reflective. Although the person using it is perfectly capable of making formal sensory-perceptual distinctions between self and world, and of testing reality in a concrete operational sense, from a psychological standpoint the language does not distinguish self from other and from world, or inner from outer reality. Under normal developmental circumstances operational reality is appreciated and dealt with appropriately and adaptively yet the psychological sense is one of a solipsistic syncretic world. Some who question the validity of postulating such a psychological state fail to appreciate this crucial distinction, because as we shall see in chapter 3, the fact is that Freud, Klein and others who formulated precursors of this process believed it is the mental operation of infancy and that it is the root of psychopathology. Critics pointed out accurately that infants and small children test reality and adapt to it well. The rub is that the meaning of reality evolves as the child's mental apparatus matures. Primordial consciousness is constructively adaptive in a supportive context, as examples throughout the book, especially in chapters 4, 7 and 8 illustrate.

Primordial consciousness is stimulus bound. It is driven by somatic sensations; evanescent affects rather than constant emotional representations, and immediate situational stimuli. It forms equally evanescent mental images rather than constant representations of ideas and related emotions. It is neither abstract nor symbolic. It is a language of motor action, body expression and sensation. Its narrative consists of images linked by affect tones and somatic sensations rather than logical sequences. As it is not reflective or recursive it does not support recognition of time passage or sequences related to memory. It does not distinguish between past and present. The absence of memory may not be apparent, as formal memory for events, experienced as concrete things, may be present, as well as the capacity for immediate recognition of something known and familiar when concretely represented, but concrete recognition of something familiar and representational remembering are not the same. It is a language of here and now rather than reflection, cogitation, and thinking about thinking. Emotions, perceptions and ideas that belong in past history are repeated as though happening in an undifferentiated present. Viewed from the lens of reflective representational thought primordial conscious mentation appears to be inconsistent, disorganized, irrational, unrealistic, impulsive and at times contradictory, but it is in fact merely the expression of a qualitatively different and potentially adaptive form of consciousness. In its proper place and context can be quite constructive and productive as we shall see in chapters 4, 6 and 7.

One of the major features of primordial consciousness and its language is syncretism. It is holistic; a language of global unity where there is no separation between self and other. As a result sensations and perceptions that might from the perspective of reflective thought be viewed as intrapsychic elements of the mind or self are instead perceived as originating in others and in the external world. It is socio-centric rather than self-centric and supports a fundamental sense of unity with others and with the cosmos rather than a sense of separateness and individuality. Because the world is animated with one's own mental content without reflective awareness, the language is one of powerful belief and conviction. It may appear from the perspective of reflective thought to be not only irrational, but when it is expressed in a context that is not socially supportive, grandiose and omnipotent. In contrast, the recursive, reflective objectification and "reality" testing, that are part of a reflective representational consciousness that distinguishes self from other and from world, necessitates a certain skepticism or questioning of the general reality and accuracy of one's ideas and recognition of the context, relativity, and the fundamental impossibility of truly knowing another and of the difference between the real world and one's subjective experience of it.

Viewed from a somewhat different perspective that I elaborate in chapter 8 on cultural differences, there are two definitions of consciousness and self-awareness. The definition most commonly accepted in Western or what I call individual-centric culture is self-consciousness or reflective awareness. What we are conscious of is what we can think about. This is the definition most generally accepted by linguists that I examine critically in chapter 5.

The other definition is of self as agent; being and doing in the world. It is the consciousness of people in tribal-spiritual or socio-centric cultures that I elaborate in chapter 8. Our consciousness is equated with our immediate experience and action regardless of whether we reflect on it. Viewed from the perspective of persons in self-centric cultures this definition of consciousness is sometimes dismissed or "studied" with names like anthropomorphism and mythology, or even delusion. From that perspective reflection is equated with maturity. Who is "right"? Each one, depending on social context. In the case of those in tribal or socio-centric cultures where the perspective is shared and socially functional it is not simply right, it is mature, regardless of whether from the perspective of persons in individual-centric cultures it seems mythological, anthropomorphic, or even delusional. Daniel Everett begins his 2008 book on the Piraha of the Amazon basin by noting an experience in which the entire tribe assembled on one bank of the river talking and gesticulating excitedly about their God whom they "saw" on the opposite bank. Of course they thought something was wrong with him and his family because they couldn't "see" it.

It is an expression of prejudice based on Western privileging of reflective representational thought to dismiss the phenomenology of primordial consciousness as irrational, disorganized, unrealistic, and even psychotic. Critics from various disciplines, including the psychoanalytic views expressed by Freud and Klein that I outline in chapter 3, and mainstream linguistics (Chomsky, 1965; Pinker, 1994), have articulated this prejudice in various ways. Psychoanalysts have equated the language of primordial consciousness with psychosis and linguists have asserted that motherese, the initial relational manifestation of primordial consciousness that is described in chapter 4, is not language because it is ungrammatical, disorganized, illogical and non-recursive. As we will see in chapter 5, the mainstream linguistic belief is that anything other than reflective representational thought does not qualify to be called language, and in the case of motherese is merely a disorganized behavioral degradation of language is mistaken. This belief is at the core of the idea that all language must contain the element of recursion. Pinker asserts that the mother-infant interchange in motherese does not teach infants language, and that it is more like animal mentation. While I agree with the second proposition, which is elaborated in subsequent chapters, in chapter 9 I offer evidence that it is the very first language, that it does facilitate development of our second language, reflective representational thought, as well, and that these two fundamental languages define our sense of self. And primordial conscious mentation is not, of itself, accompanied by any cognitive sensory-perceptual failure or inability to navigate in the world, as for example blindness or deafness. As a matter of fact, infantile perception and functional response to "reality" is quite accurate and functionally adaptive. Whatever meaning infants assign to the perceptions is another matter.

How expressions of primordial consciousness are perceived and the consequences of its use depend upon the congruence or lack thereof with the interpersonal, social and cultural context of the individual; that is, whether the context does or does not normalize and support such mental activity. Primordial consciousness is simply a different way of organizing self and cosmos, one that can be constructive and creative, or disturbed and pathological, depending both on the context in which it is used, and on its relationship to reflective representational thought. In chapters 7, 8 and 10 I offer examples to clarify this distinction.

Primordial consciousness, the mother tongue, is not transformed into or superseded by reflective representational symbolic thought. It is a separate entity not a developmental stage and its potential remains throughout life, even though, in some settings that strongly favor reflective representational logical thought, its phenomenological manifestations are scarce. Rather, maturation of the brain and social development enable acquisition of reflective symbolic consciousness, and the two forms of consciousness coexist in potential and in varying proportions depending both on the idiosyncrasies of each individual's development and the mores of the cultural, interpersonal and social surroundings.

Chapter 3
Theoretical background of the problem of mental process and consciousness

I would like to examine two major theoretical root systems underlying my hypothesis of two qualitatively different kinds of conscious mental activity each with its unique use of the formal aspects of language. The first is neuropsychological and the second is psychoanalytic, and they are personified by Julian Jaynes on the one hand and Freud and Melanie Klein on the other.

Julian Jaynes and the model of the bicameral mind

The discovery of basic differences in right and left cerebral hemisphere functioning by Nobel Prize laureate Roger Sperry (1961) in cooperation with Michael Gazzaniga (1967) provided the neuroscience background for Julian Jaynes's (1976) classic work *The Origin of Consciousness*. Sperry and Gazzaniga studied patients whose corpus callosum had been surgically severed as treatment for intractable epilepsy. They discovered that hemispheric function was related to handedness, and that in right-handed individuals the left hemisphere specialized in analytical thinking and language whereas the right hemisphere tended to be sensory, emotional, impressionistic and spatial.

In 1976 Jaynes published the evolutionary hypothesis known as bicameralism in which he outlined two qualitatively distinctive forms of mental activity and their putative neurological underpinnings. He hypothesized that humankind evolved within the past 3000 years from a disconnected unconscious state of domination by the right hemisphere that he called the bicameral mind. His descriptions of ancient and tribal human mind and of schizophrenia depict the right brain domination he ascribes to the bicameral state. In primitive humans he emphasizes anthropomorphism; undifferentiation of mind and cosmos characterized by mythologies and God beliefs, as well as the absence of ability to reflect or introspect about mind that he finds characteristic of action mythologies such as *Iliad* and *Odyssey*. His description of schizophrenia is also "bicameral." He describes auditory hallucinations commanding action, the absence of a sense of separate self capable of reflecting on one's mind that he calls "the analog I," and the related inability to construct a realistic, logical narrative about self that he calls "narratization."

Translated into the terminology of the model I have proposed, the mental functions he attributes to the right hemisphere include undifferentiation of mind from external reality; loss of the capacity to reflect and introspect; and loss of realistic logic, all of which are elements of the mental activity of primordial consciousness that I described in chapter 2. He maintained that in the course of Darwinian evolution and the need to adapt to increasingly complex social structures characteristic of the modern world the corpus callosum evolved and enabled communication between the hemispheres, enabling humans to become psychologically conscious. Along with Descartes and like Freud, he assumed a single-minded consciousness that is based on self-awareness, reflection and introspection. He defined conscious thought as the capacity to differentiate inside from outside, and the acquisition of selective control over behavior based upon reflective thought. He believed that consciousness comes after language and is based on it (1976, p. 66) but he does not seem to find a place in his theory for the fact that the data of ancient writings from Greece and the Old Testament from which he deduces unconscious mind are highly verbal.

With the hypothesis of a primitive mind that had not yet differentiated itself and become conscious Jaynes accounted for the non-reflective mythopoetically dominated mental state he believed from written accounts to be characteristic of ancient Greece, the Old Testament Bible, and tribal humankind. He further postulated that mental states characteristic of religion, cultism, schizophrenia, and other extreme belief systems are leftovers or "vestiges" of the earlier unconscious bicameral state.

His division of two qualitatively distinctive mental processes bears remarkable similarity to Freud's psychoanalytically based model of the primary and secondary processes, and his hypothesis of the relationship of the primary process to schizophrenia. Jaynes's ideas are also similar to the divisions I propose between primordial consciousness and reflective representational thought.

Although Jaynes's work has retained a loyal following it has been mostly discredited based on apparent flaws in his understanding of brain function. Jaynes's neurobiological hypothesis has been widely criticized (Moffic, 1987), and within neurology gross hypotheses involving lateralization of function have largely been replaced with the more sophisticated concept of neural circuitry. And there is no substantial evidence to support (or refute) his evolutionary hypothesis. Although it is true that "lower" primates and animals do seem to function based on primordial consciousness, as I mentioned in chapter 2, the reason would appear to be that they lack the frontal lobe capacity for language and related reasoning rather than that they lack a functioning connection between existing parts of the brain. I believe the most important reason for the dismissal of Jaynes's work is spurious. It is the failure to separate his insights into mental function from his neurological and evolutionary hypothesis and to recognize that his insights into mind can stand on their own, and are not dependent on the validity of his hypotheses about brain and evolution (Dennett, 1986). In the bigger picture there is remarkable congruence between his ideas about mind,

Freud's model of the primary and secondary processes, and the hypothesis about mental process, consciousness and language that I present. I refer to this in subsequent phenomenological sections of the book.

Sigmund Freud and the primary process

The name behind the psychoanalytic contribution is Sigmund Freud. In his classic, *The Interpretation of Dreams* (1900a), he proposed two basic mental processes, the primary process, which he believed to be unconscious, and the secondary process of ordinary conscious thought. Melanie Klein subsequently proposed the model of the paranoid-schizoid position and phantasy, which bears more similarity to Freud's model of the primary process than most people seem to realize.

Freud's model of the primary process is the theoretical root of my hypothesis of primordial consciousness. Freud seems not to have realized the revolutionary nature of his discovery, that he was conceptualizing a normal form of conscious mental activity that is qualitatively different from reflective representational thought. He vacillated between describing the primary process as invisible to direct conscious awareness (unconscious) and as an arcane variant of ordinary symbolic thought, and he vacillated as to whether the process is normal or abnormal (Robbins, 2011, 2015, 2018).

Freud's prototypical data for the existence of a primary mental process is the phenomenology of dreaming. Freud described dreaming as the royal road to the aspect of mind that is unconscious or invisible. In other words, he believed that its mental structure or fabric which he described as the primary process is unconscious because we are not aware of it. That is, we cannot know it as part of reflective thought. I propose a way of looking at it in which the primary process is the road to or the structure of a mental process of which we are consciously aware in a manner different from reflective representational thought (Robbins, 2015). Possibly some of the reason Freud labelled the process unconscious is that his prototypical mental activity, dreaming, occurs in a state of *physiological* unconsciousness in which the mind is periodically active but the motor system is paralyzed. It is important to distinguish this state from psychological unconsciousness, and as we shall see, Freud was not able to do this though he attempted to do so by proposing an ambiguous state he called preconsciousness.

Freud concluded that dreams are the sensory-perceptual actualizations of a mind momentarily unfettered by waking conscious awareness of social reality or by the potential consequences of uncontrolled action were the motor system not restrained. He believed this state that he called unconsciousness was one in which, lacking reflection and reality checking, wishes can be believed to come true, therefore he called the governing motivation the pleasure principle. The process is characterized by displacement, condensation, and absence of contradiction. It creates sensory-perceptual identity or a sense of reality related to hallucination and delusion in waking life. In other words, a major feature of the primary process is absence of differentiation between mind and world. The primary process creates a narrative sequence by affective (instinctual) association of images rather than by reality-governed logic and temporal causality. In contrasting the primary process with wakeful consciousness he states, "The primary process endeavours to bring about a discharge of excitation in order that ... it may establish a 'perceptual identity.' The secondary process, however, has abandoned this intention and taken on another in its place – the establishment of a 'thought identity'" (1900a, p. 602). He adds that the subjective experience of the dreamer is not one of thought but "a complete hallucinatory cathexis of the perceptual systems" (p. 548). And "the dream-work proper diverges further from our picture of waking thought than has been supposed ... it is completely different from it qualitatively and for that reason not immediately comparable with it" (p. 507). He elaborates the differences between dreaming and reflective representational thought: "One is the fact that the thought is represented as an immediate situation with the 'perhaps' omitted, and the other is the fact that the thought is transformed into visual images and speech" (p. 534). After describing the primary process Freud later made the fateful and questionable leap of reason that "These are the characteristics we may expect to find in processes belonging to the system Ucs." (1915e, p. 187).

Freud called the mental process primary because he believed it is the ontologically first process, the mind of infancy prior to awareness of reality. He wrote that "... the infant ... probably hallucinates the fulfilment of its internal needs; it betrays its unpleasure when there is an increase of stimulus and an absence of satisfaction, by the motor discharge of screaming and beating about with its arms and legs, and it then experiences the satisfaction it has hallucinated" (1911b, p. 218 fn.). In the process of growth and adaptation based on the reality principle, the secondary system or process, conscious reflective thought, develops. Many since Freud have questioned Freud's assumption that the infant mind is unconscious and unrealistic, citing evidence that infants adapt to reality in a different way utilizing the conscious processes available to them. However, by equating consciousness with waking reflective representational thought Freud was able to reason that the primary process is unconscious. Other conclusions follow from this path of reasoning such as because the primary process is unconscious its presence cannot be observed directly but must be inferred. He equated the mental process in dreaming with that of symptom formation, reasoned that symptoms are also manifestations of unconscious mind and phenomenological reflections of the primary process, and in order to account for their formation he introduced the concept of dynamic repression.

I speculate that much of the ambiguity and confusion that I have outlined resulted because Freud was not fully able to appreciate the profundity of his discovery of a qualitatively different mental process and its role in mental life. Otherwise perhaps he would have focused more of his work on the severe psychoses and on other phenomena of everyday that I will describe subsequently, as he remarks in several places that they are manifestations of the primary process. Instead of fully embracing that conclusion and its implications for mind he retreated in various writings and contradicted himself by making the more conservative argument that the primary process is just an arcane version of reflective symbolic thought. In a number of places he articulated his belief that the structure of dreams is qualitatively similar to that of thought, implying that it is not necessary to postulate a qualitatively distinctive mental process to comprehend. Had he gone so far as to make the obvious conclusion that dreaming is a variant of conscious mind not an absence of it he would have had to question his belief that the primary process is unconscious and he would have had to make a clearer distinction between physiological wakefulness and psychological consciousness. He writes: "... dreams appear to engage in making symbolic representations of the body, we now know that those representations are the product of certain unconscious phantasies..." (1900a, p. 612). Without realizing he was implying dreaming is a conscious activity he used the analogy of different languages to describe the difference between dreams and waking thoughts. In the same work we read that:

> The dream-thoughts and the dream-content are presented to us like two versions of the same subject-matter in two different languages. Or, more properly, the dream-content seems like a transcript of the dream-thoughts into another mode of expression, whose characters and syntactic laws it is our business to discover by comparing the original and the translation. The dream-thoughts are immediately comprehensible, as soon as we have learnt them. The dream-content, on the other hand, is expressed as it were in a pictographic script, the characters of which have to be transposed individually into the language of the dream-thoughts. (1900a, p. 277)

He notes that "the productions of the dream-work, which, it must be remembered, are not made with the intention of being understood, present no greater difficulties to their translators than do the ancient hieroglyphic scripts to those who seek to read them," and "... the keys are generally known and laid down by firmly established linguistic usage" (pp. 341–342). In summary, at the same time that Freud maintained that language is used by the primary process concretely and literally as a thing of action (for example the use of expletives) in a primary process qualitatively different from logical symbolic thought, he also believed that the language of dreaming is an arcane form of symbolism that can be decoded by the same associative language principles that apply to ordinary language.

Freud did consider another possibility in his effort to resolve ambiguity and confusion of which he must have been partly aware, namely that dreaming in particular and the primary process in general might be conscious albeit in a different way than that of reflective symbolic thought. In proposing another mental process, the preconscious, he suggested the possibility of concrete evanescent affect-driven imagery different from constant abstract representation.

He writes: "A very great part of this preconscious originates in the unconscious, has the character of its derivatives and is subjected to a censorship before it can become conscious. Another part of the Pcs. is capable of becoming conscious without any censorship" (1915e, p. 190). System Pcs. is characterized as an intermediate censor that partakes of both systems at different times. It seems confusing to describe dreaming both as a primary process function and as a preconscious one. But perhaps the concept of preconscious was Freud's embryonic effort to describe another form of consciousness with characteristics such as evanescent imagery different from those of reflective symbolic thought.

Before turning to the work of Melanie Klein, I briefly mention Jung's (1912) contribution to the attempt to articulate a mental process different from ordinary thought. He proposed a mental activity that is similar to the primary process and to what I describe shortly as Klein's contribution, phantasy, but in contrast to the confusion in their writings he was clear in his belief that it is mature and constructive, reflecting the spirituality and creativity of humankind. However, he also viewed it as unconscious, perhaps because of its relationship to dreaming. And he chose concepts to describe it such as "irresponsible thinking" that do not entirely escape the implication of pathology. He was perhaps the first to note the relationship of this process to culture, and to describe how it characterizes tribal/spiritual cultures, a connection that Jaynes (1976) noted as well, and that I elaborate in chapter 8. He described it as a way of seeing the world in accord with one's wishes rather than objective reality, and he viewed this more as creative than pathological.

Although Klein and her followers did not recognize and acknowledge their debt to Freud, perhaps because of the contentious political atmosphere that culminated in the so-called "Controversial Discussions" in the UK during WWII, they also struggled to articulate another form of mental activity. Klein postulated the unintegrated and undifferentiated paranoid-schizoid position. Whereas dreaming served as Freud's basic data from which to understand the nature of unconscious mind, Klein used children's play. Recall that Freud used the term "primary" because he believed the process characterized infancy, and presumably early childhood. While there is no reference to the primary process in Klein's writings, in 1946 Klein conjoined her concept of phantasy, the mental process of the paranoid-schizoid position, with the adjective "unconscious." Most of the references to phantasy of Susan Isaacs, as well as those of Hanna Segal, Klein's most important explicators, are similarly coupled with the adjective "unconscious."

Isaacs (1948) offers a particularly eloquent description of phantasy as a somatic process different from and antecedent to conceptual thought. It is concrete and enactive rather than symbolic and reflective, sensory-perceptual-somatic-motor, undifferentiated and unintegrated in the sense implied by projective identification. It creates a hallucinatory-delusional sense of actualization. The mind of phantasy is somatic; gastrointestinal and urogenital; based on the belief that what is "good" can be ingested and what is "bad" can be excreted or eliminated. Need is experienced and enacted orally as somatic tropism toward the mother (breast) that is undifferentiated from a state of satisfaction (goodness), and frustration elicits somatic-psychic excretory responses that are equally undifferentiated from parts of the object (badness). States of incipient and actual satisfaction are experienced as an omnipotent (undifferentiated) hallucinatory-delusional belief that Klein named the "good" breast, while states of frustration and rage are projectively identified in the other as belief in a destroyed/destroying (persecutory) "bad" breast. In contrast to Klein and most Kleinians Isaacs acknowledges that:

> The earliest and most rudimentary phantasies, bound up with sensory experience, and being affective interpretations of bodily sensations, are naturally characterized by those qualities which Freud described as belonging to the "primary process": lack of co-ordination of impulse, lack of sense of time, of contradiction, and of negation. Furthermore, at this level, there is no discrimination of external reality. Experience is governed by "all or none" responses and the absence of satisfaction is felt as a positive evil. Loss, dissatisfaction or deprivation are felt in sensation to be positive, painful experiences. (1948, p. 87)

I noted that Freud's conception of preconsciousness might have been an effort to deal with the question of whether the "other" mental activity is conscious, albeit in a different way. Klein (1930) made a similar effort when she followed in the footsteps of Jones (1918) and coined the concept of symbolic equation. The term is meant to describe a mental process that simultaneously partakes of qualities of concreteness and symbolism. Segal, in a series of papers (1957, 1978, 1994), addressed this seeming paradox as follows:

> ... there is a distinction between concrete symbolism, in which the symbol is equated with what is symbolised, and a more evolved form, in which the symbol represents the object but is not confused and identified with it, and does not lose its own characteristics. Concrete symbolism leads to misperception and false beliefs. (1994, p. 395)

Ronald Britton (1998), one of the most influential contemporary Kleinians, has gone a step further and states that the paranoid-schizoid position, and presumably fantasy, is actually a qualitatively different form of conscious mentation. The oxymoronic concept of symbolic equation might better be replaced with a concept of concrete, situational or stimulus-bound, affect or impulse-driven imagery.

The confusion in Klein's attempt to distinguish between phantasy as a qualitatively different mental activity from *fantasy*, which is an aspect of conscious symbolic thought, is illustrated by her choice of the language of *fantasy* to describe it. She used the language of reflective differentiated symbolic thought about body parts, distinctions between goodness and badness, conflicts and defenses over emotional states of rage and desire. In other words, it is the language of conscious *fantasy*. The confusion is also illustrated by the contradictory concept of symbolic equation. Klein's use of the language of fantasy, a product of reflective representational thought, to describe phantasy, a primary process-like activity, reflects her confusion. The linguistic assumption by the Kleinian analyst that *phantasy* is *fantasy* can lead to significant relational miscommunication and may be responsible for the sense some have that the classical Kleinian technique is not collaborative and empathic. The unwitting assumption behind some Kleinian interpretations in the language of fantasy is that the patient can think about activity that has all the qualities of the primary process or phantasy in symbolic thoughtful language. This assumption ignores the essential cognitive problem that the patient needs help to translate from one form of mental activity to another.

I mention without elaboration one other significant effort to distinguish two mental processes. Matte-Blanco (1975, 1988) described two forms of logic (his term for mental activity) that he called asymmetric and symmetric. Asymmetric logic is the equivalent of reflective recursive thought. His description of symmetric logic bears much resemblance to Freud's primary process. Like Freud, he believed it to be unconscious, only inferable by its effects on asymmetric logic, even though the process he described is directly observable.

In recent years theorists with relational and attachment theory orientations have produced a substantial literature designed to explicate the area of mental life Freud referred to as unconscious processes that is not defensively repressed but is not available to reflective conscious awareness. For the most part this group has described the relevant processes in terms of absence of symbolic representation of somatic-motoric-sensory-perceptual experience; what the body knows but the mind has not grasped and articulated. Numerous conceptual labels have been used, the most common being implicit or procedural knowledge. From this large literature I extract several representative contributions. The Boston Change Process Study Group (BCPSG) (2007) describes implicit or procedural knowing as follows:

> ... we are not referring to the infant's cognitive function, but to the way that physiological and then social/behavioral regulation is carried out between the infant and its caregiver, and represented and "remembered" by the infant ... [it] ... guides the moment-to-moment exchanges that occur in any interaction ... such as gestures, vocalizations, silences and rhythms. (p. 844)

They go on to say that "... relational knowing is thus a form of representation ... [but] ... we do not imply a symbolic process" (p. 844). Lyons-Ruth, an attachment theorist, writes:

> ... if development is not primarily about translating primary process into symbolic form, but about developing implicit adaptive procedures for being with others in a wide range of emotionally charged situations, then making

the unconscious conscious does not adequately describe developmental or psychoanalytic change. (1999, p. 589)

An implication is that there is a void where mind could be, that the processes involved are somatic and behavioral, representational in the sense of concrete and imagistic, passive and reflexive. Stern et al. (1998), describe implicit "... knowing about interpersonal and intersubjective relations, i.e. how to be with someone . . . Such *knowings* integrate affect, cognition, and behavioural/interactive dimensions" (p. 903).

Emde (1993) states that:

> There is a major amount of nonconscious mental activity that is neither preconscious (i.e., readily accessible to consciousness using recent or working memory) nor defensively excluded (i.e., involving repressed memories or isolated affects) . . . a variety of organized automatically functioning procedures and rules for guiding behavior in particular contexts. (p. 415)

These contributions continue to reflect the ambiguity about whether the process is unconscious, conscious in a concrete, stimulus bound, imagistic manner, or conscious in the form of reflective symbolic thought, at the same time that they are a valuable corrective to the tendency to equate unconsciousness with repression, immaturity and pathology. However, they direct attention to a kind of mental void; behavioral automatisms in the absence of reflective symbolic consciousness rather than the idea of an active and complex conscious mental process that is different from reflective representational thought.

Wilma Bucci (1997, 2000, 2011) addressed this problem and formulated a three level hierarchy consisting of sub-symbolic nonverbal processing, nonverbal symbolic processing, and verbal symbolic thought. Her model of sub-symbolic process encompasses the area of imagistic consciousness. She also describes sub-symbolic processes using some of the same terminology as primary process – concrete, nonverbal, sensory-perceptual-motor, and analogical. In seeming contradiction she describes the process as chaotic rather than lawful and organized, whereas it seems to follow from her own descriptions that it is an orderly process albeit one that is different from reflective thought.

The primary process, derived from the study of dreaming, may have been Freud's most profound contribution to the study of mind, although he was not bold enough to embrace its radical implications. He does not seem to have been completely satisfied with his conclusion that it is the foundation of unconscious mental processes. I believe what he was on the verge of realizing is that it is the basis of a model of conscious mind qualitatively different from reflective representational thought that is the underpinning of many mental phenomena ranging from dreaming, to psychosis, and including creativity, belief systems, parent-infant bonding, cultural differences, and more.

Chapter 4

Fundamental manifestations of primordial consciousness
Dreaming and the languages of mother-infant bonding

Dreaming is the initial and quintessential expression of primordial consciousness activity. It is also its purest form of expression as it occurs in a state of physiological unconsciousness under circumstances (sleep) when motor paralysis prevents action; except for those unusual individuals who possess the capacity for lucid dreaming, there is no competition from waking thought. It is misleading, however, to conclude, as did Freud, that because dreaming occurs in a physiologically unconscious state that the activity itself is unconscious. From a psychological not a physiological perspective dreaming is a conscious activity, albeit in a manner different from the consciousness of reflective symbolic thought.

The major but apparently not exclusive neurological substrate of dreaming, the REM state, has been recorded *in utero* as early as seven months, even before rapid eye movements commence (Schwab, Groh, Schwab, & Witte, 2009). Some infants are able to indicate shortly after they begin to speak that they have dreams, as Freud documented in his daughter Anna's sleep-talking about strawberries at 19 months of age. Primordial consciousness is the mental operation at a time when reflective thought is as yet relatively undeveloped due to a combination of lack of socialization and the delayed myelination of critical aspects of brain (Paus et al., 1999).

Primordial consciousness and the language with which it is expressed is the "mother tongue" because it is the first mental process and because it is the first socialization. It is the avenue by which mother and infant become attached or bonded. At the beginning of the third trimester of intrauterine life the fetal brain becomes capable of REM sleep and the neurological capacity for communication, the capacity for hearing, comes on line. At this time aural interactions between mother and infant commence so that at birth the infant demonstrates a selective tropism toward mother's voice. Darwin (1871) described the relationship between musicality, bonding and the acquisition of language and stated that musical communication preceded the formal aspects of language acquisition. In the last trimester the dyadic interaction is musical or prosodic. Maternal sounds and the words and sentences that accompany them elicit physical/neurological fetal responses. After birth both parties contribute gestures, facial expressions and musical sounds to the attachment experience. New parents are often surprised to find themselves in reflexively synchronized vocal-facial-gestural-expressive interactions with their infants: interactions that they might not want adults outside the family to witness lest they be thought to have lost their minds. The language has been called "motherese" (Durkin, Rutter & Tucker, 1982; Fernald & Kuhl, 1987; Fernald & Simon, 1984; Grieser & Kuhl, 1988), IDL (infant directed language), and what is known colloquially as "baby talk." The mother tongue is universal and transcends any particular language. Ferguson (1964) documented its presence in six different language speaking countries. Fathers and other caregivers do it as well, but the unique bond is forged with the mother as it begins *in utero*.

It is worthy of note that REM sleep and the process of dreaming that it supports do not appear to be unique to humans. Dog lovers often tell stories of behaviors their pets manifest during sleep from which one can infer the presence of dreaming. REM sleep has been documented in terrestrial placental mammals and in birds as well (Capellini, Preston, McNamara, Barton, & Nunn, 2009). Hence we can infer that primordial consciousness is not an exclusively human attribute but is found in most animals and birds as well: a conclusion consistent with observations of their "intelligent" interactions with humans and with one another. Burnham, Kitamura & Vollmer-Conna (2002) compared how mothers interact vocally with their six month olds to interaction with their pets and found great similarity. The feature that distinguishes human interaction with infants from interaction with animals is the presence of hyper-articulation of words, supporting the hypothesis that what differentiates primordial consciousness in humans from that of animals is the presence of language capability.

In these initial interactions mother is teaching her infant the language with which to express primordial consciousness. While the potential for primordial consciousness continues throughout life, there is research evidence that it is a unique form of interaction that more or less concludes by the end of the first year of life, certainly by age 5 or so, and that it sets the stage for the qualitatively different process of learning reflective representational thought that ensues in later infancy and childhood. A more extensive discussion of these processes will be found in chapter 9 on the emergence of language and the sense of self during the attachment phase.

Returning to dreaming and primordial consciousness, dreams are not reflective or recursive. During the dream proper we do not have the capacity to remember what came before the instant moment in a dream. That kind of reconstruction has to wait until the wakened dreamer struggles to cast the images and sequences into reflective representational thought and tries to reconstruct a sequence of events and their linkage. There is no differentiation between internal and external or between reality and fantasy. However the dream images are expressed in terms of self and others in the language of waking life into which the dream is cast, all the characters and actions are undifferentiated aspects of the dreamer's mind. The imagistic narrative is driven by affects, not rationality and logic, so that from the perspective of waking reflective thought it seems fragmented and disorganized. It would lead to unchecked action were it not for the fact that the motor system is paralyzed, which is one of the reasons Freud concluded dreaming is the mental activity of delusional and hallucinatory psychosis.

Dreams are characterized by nonsymbolic (concrete) evanescent images and sequences determined by the predominant affect(s) associated with them. Such imagery has been mistaken for symbolism (Robbins, 2015) because on awakening the dreamer moves into the realm of reflective representational thought, recasts the dream images into the abstract language of symbolism, and uses the recursive memory function that is lacking in the dream itself. If one is not clear about the distinction between the dream proper and the waking rendition it is easy to make the fallacious assumption that it is recursive and contains symbolic references to a deeper layer of meaning.

The difference between imagistic and symbolic mentation in dreaming was vividly illustrated in my work with Jacob, whose essay on his own use of language will be found in chapter 17. For some years of our early work, as he comments, he presented to me vivid images from his childhood relationship with his mother. To him they just "were" and we clashed when he shared them because I interpreted them as statements of his relationship with her but to him they were just images, although he presented them repeatedly. My receptive thought as an observer able to abstract representational meaning and infer appropriate emotional responses from these images, was that he was telling me about his memories of his mother's abusive treatment of him as a small child – repeatedly sticking her fingers and other things up his rectum in search of something "wrong" with him; using the flimsiest of excuses to find something "wrong" with him and calling doctors to give him multiple tests; stripping him naked in public, once again with flimsy excuses; telling him about the horrible episiotomy he had caused her to have at his birth, and much, much more. But when I would comment on her abusive treatment and wonder about his anger and hurt he would become violently angry at me, as in his mind these images did not add up to a constant emotional representation of being abused and angry, and because his mother had used the language of love to define their relationship, and had told him that she loved him. He would accuse me of trying to take over his mind, something that in a sense had a grain of truth to it and that he expressed somatically with such phrases as making him "suck up," or trying to suffocate him. That his behavior was not defensive against repressed knowledge is eloquently indicated in his essay, where he writes of how he literally did not know the more abstract significance of his imagery because he was unable at that time to represent and be aware of his own emotions. In other words, it takes reflective representational thought, supportive of symbolization, to find deeper meaning in the sequences presented in primordially conscious images, whether waking or in dreams.

Chapter 5

The relation of mental process and language
The controversy within linguistics

Language reflects and expresses mental process, although as I argue in chapter 6, the two are not isomorphic. The currently most popular linguistic theory poses a major obstacle to the hypothesis I have proposed that there are two qualitatively distinctive mental activities each of which uses language differently, and that one of them, primordial consciousness, does not include reflection or recursion. The dominant linguistic theory known as universal or generative grammar and developed by Noam Chomsky, postulates that there is but a single language template, generated genetically, and that recursion is its clearest defining feature. No recursion, then no language, despite how many words and efforts at sentences there may be.

Like so many other aspects of personality, language expresses both our genetic uniqueness and our responses to the interpersonal, social and cultural environment into which we are born. Language has been conceptualized reductively by those who believe the theory of generative grammar as a system more or less like a physical appendage, whose form and function unfold in predetermined invariant ways from neurological givens common to all humans. These theorists generally recognize that semantic elements, some of the specifics of content and employment will depend on the social and developmental context of the bearer, much like our arms may differ in various characteristics depending upon whether we grow up to work in a coal mine or teach at a university. In chapter 2 I proposed a different hypothesis, that language is not a monolithic entity but that there are two fundamental human language templates.

The theory of universal grammar, attributable to Noam Chomsky (Hauser, Chomsky & Fitch, 2002) is that there are invariant biologically based characteristics that all languages, regardless of their superficial differences related to grammar, vocabulary and semantics, share and that set humans apart from other animals. The Chomsky group concludes that the mechanism called recursion is the visible lynchpin of the biological template. Therefore there can be no language that lacks recursion. The Chomsky group disqualifies what I described in chapter 2 as "motherese," the partially verbal interaction of mothers with their infants, as legitimate language, as it lacks recursion and by their standards for language is disorganized. They also challenge evidence that I outline next that there are peoples whose language lacks recursion.

The linguistic anthropologist Daniel Everett (2008) believes that there are languages that lack recursion, and takes the further step to assert that this means language is basically a social product relative to one's indigenous context rather than an entity that is biologically constrained. I believe that the controversy is based on the Cartesian assumption that equates language and consciousness with reflection or recursion, leading to the false premise that language is monolithic, and on a failure to appreciate that mind works in two qualitatively distinctive ways, each of which makes idiosyncratic use of language. This distinction is the foundation for the hypothesis that significant human behavior, both constructive and pathological, including major language aberrations, can be understood as reflections of primordial consciousness that has a language of its own distinct from reflective representational thought.

Proponents of the physical reductive view of language known as generative grammar cluster at MIT. Its creator and champion is Noam Chomsky (1959, 1965), and one of Chomsky's disciples is Steven Pinker (1994), who wrote about what he called the language instinct. The idea is that language is a monolithic entity, the physical product of innate or deep structure in the brain, and that like our arms and legs, while life experiences may affect their form and function, the basic elements or "rules" of function are predetermined and immutable. Infants are hypothesized to be pre-wired with innate knowledge about the structure of language and need only learn the idiosyncratic features of the language(s) they are exposed to in order to generate an infinity of comprehensible utterances. The developmental importance of early mother-infant interaction in language learning is discounted by this group, along with the possibility that the mother tongue is part of a distinctive language system. Wilson and Weinstein remark:

> These [Chomskian] linguists stress a multilevel "hard-wired" perspective on language acquisition in children. Their view proposes invariant or universal aspects of language development as an essential aspect of brain maturation, independent of and/or prior to the input of earliest social phenomena. This stance led to a relative de-emphasis of individual differences and the more microscopic elements of object-relating in language acquisition.
> (1992, p. 351)

Chomsky's position is sometimes misrepresented by exaggeration as completely discounting the role of environment, culture and learning in the development of language. That is not the case. It is more accurate to say that the role of socialization is limited to the more superficial aspects of language. In 1965 he added a semantic component to the previous largely syntactical emphasis of grammatical rules. The new version of transformational grammar includes not only syntactical rules for generating sentences but also semantic rules governing the assignment of meaning to such sentences. As he put it:

Thus the syntactic component consists of a base that generates deep structures and a transformational part that maps them into surface structures. The deep structure of a sentence is submitted to the semantic component for semantic interpretation, and its surface structure enters the phonological component and undergoes phonetic interpretation. The final effect of a grammar, then, is to relate a semantic interpretation to a phonetic representation, that is, to state how a sentence is interpreted. This relation is mediated by the syntactic component of the grammar, which constitutes its sole "creative" part." (1965, pp. 135–136)

In 1978 he writes:

Surely the normal use of language requires access to other systems of knowledge and belief . . . We use language against a background of shared beliefs about things and within the framework of a system of social institutions. The study of language use must be concerned with the place of language in a system of cognitive structures embodying pragmatic competence, as well as structures that relate to matters of fact and belief. (p. 35)

From the perspective of believing that language is a monolithic entity, however, Chomsky discounts phenomena which illustrate that there are two qualitatively different forms of language. Before proceeding further I want to make clear that my linguistic background does not qualify me as expert on the nuances of the controversy within linguistics nor do I have space to do justice to the arguments on each side of what has become a heated, even acrimonious debate between members of the Cognitive Science Department at MIT and various others, including defectors from that camp. However, I think there is a key element of relevance to the debate that both sides have overlooked.

Recursion is a concept basic to mathematics, found, for example in the systematically repetitive characteristic of the Fibonacci sequence, and in philosophy, for example, in Descartes's writings. Statements of his such as "cogito, ergo sum" and "I doubt, therefore I think, therefore I am," imply thinking about thinking. Recursion is found in such things as relativity, reflection, feedback, subsets and imbeddedness. It is related to the ability to compare and contrast, perceive similarity and contradiction, and hence it is an essential characteristic of reflective representational thought.

Chomsky (Hauser, Chomsky & Fitch, 2002) claims that recursion is a necessary feature of language, and perhaps the uniquely human feature of mind that distinguishes it from the undoubted purposeful and otherwise seemingly intelligent mental activity of terrestrial placental mammals and birds. In an article in the *Boston Globe* (January 25, 2017) titled "10 ways that animals are smarter than you think," Deborah Halber writes about the work of Irene Pepperberg, who claims that parrots, among other species, have cognitive abilities similar to those of small children. The eponymous parrot uttering "Polly want a cracker" may actually have a concrete image (not a symbolic representation) of a cracker, but is not capable of saying "John, the sailor who bought me on the Pacific Island, taught me to say 'Polly want a cracker.'" Or "That cracker I had yesterday was so good I'd like another." Pinker states that recursion is a procedure that invokes an instance of itself: ". . . all you need for recursion is an ability to embed a noun phrase within a noun phrase, or a clause within a clause . . ." (1994, p. 379). For example, a sentence can have a structure in which what follows the verb is another sentence: "John believes that the Republicans will win the election." Or, "John remembered that he had forgotten to shave this morning." Daniel Everett (2008) describes recursion as a self-referential process. The capacity for recursion, as it relates to language and thought, is essential to the uniquely human quality of memory as a mental activity, distinguished from the animal capacity for recognition on confrontation of something that is familiar. Recognition and memory are different although the immediate behavioral consequences may appear to be the same.

Everett (2008), whose professional evolution from missionary to the Piraha tribe in the Amazon basin to cultural anthropologist and linguist is a story in itself, claims the language of the Piraha lacks recursion, and describes other features that seem to distinguish it and their mental process from the norms of most – certainly Western – languages. However, he does not take the further step of hypothesizing what the difference may signify for language. His observations are recounted in some detail in chapter 8. Piraha language is characterized by repetition, reiteration and contiguity, based on the concept of immediacy, now is everything; it does not distinguish time past, present, or future. Based on observations such as this, Everett challenges not only the particular claim of the Chomsky group but the underlying reductionist neurobiological assumption that spawned it, and suggests that discovery of a language lacking recursion is evidence that language is largely determined by the particulars of context and culture. While I agree with Everett's conclusion about recursion, both extreme opposite assumptions may be mistaken; that of the Chomsky group that there is a single template for language and that recursion is its central feature, and that of Everett and his supporters that finding languages not based on recursion means that language is basically culturally determined.

With increasing understanding of the human brain, the principle of neural plasticity, and the reciprocal interaction of brain and experience, it seems as with so many things that the answer is to be found not at either extreme but in interaction between nature and nurture. In the ensuing discussion I advance evidence to show that mind, whose substrate is brain, works in two qualitatively different ways, one of which uses language in a way that conforms to the principle of recursion and the other that does not. Where socialization and culture fit in the picture is that they preferentially encourage or discourage one or the other of these mental processes. The results include a linguistic mix within some cultures and social groups as well as extremes of cultures whose linguistic expressions are predominantly recursive and others that are not.

Chapter 6

The relationship of language to thought and the sense of self

Another heated controversy within linguistics, cognitive science and philosophy has to do with the relationship of language to thought, both of which are intimately related to one's sense of self. Are language and thought isomorphic? Are they distinctive but related? What does development have to inform us about their relationship?

In an extensive review of this literature Meissner (2008) concluded that thought, language and speech are not identical. The major authority on this subject is probably Lev Vygotsky, who writes, "Thought has its own structure, and the transition from it to speech is no easy matter" (1962, p. 208). Vygotsky used a kind of Venn diagram analogy in which he compared thought and speech to two intersecting circles, in which the overlapping part represented verbal thought. He claims that "The structure of speech does not simply mirror the structure of thought; that is why words cannot be put on by thought like a ready-made garment. Thought undergoes many changes as it turns into speech" (1962, p. 126). Elsewhere he writes:

> The structure of speech is not a simple mirror image of the structure of thought. It cannot, therefore, be placed on thought like clothes off a rack. Speech does not merely serve as an expression of developed thought. Thought is restructured as it is transformed in speech. It is not expressed but completed in the word. (1987, p. 251)

Vygotsky believed that language is a social development, integrally related to communication with another person. In the course of development the process of language development diverges. One path leads to further acquisition of social communication; the other involves the internalization of language through a progressive movement from social speech through egocentric speech to private inner speech. This latter process is part of the development of thought. Of particular relevance to the model of two qualitatively different forms of consciousness he writes: "A word is a microcosm of human consciousness" (1934, p. 256).

Stern and the Boston Change Process Study Group examined preverbal interactions between mother and infant and concluded that what they call thinking is present well before the acquisition of language. They point to patterns of mutual interaction and coordination between mother and child and conclude that "Infants are born with minds that are especially attuned to other minds as manifest through their behavior" (2004, p. 648). Their implicit assumption that there is but one conscious mental process that they call thought seems similar to that of the Chomsky group that I summarized in the last chapter. Paradoxically the mental process they describe also resembles the animal mentation related to primordial consciousness that I summarized in the last chapter. Bucci (1997) entertains a somewhat different hypothesis that in some respects resembles the one I have proposed. She claims that language and thought evolve along different pathways and are eventually integrated so that much of thought can be expressed in words and speech. In other words, the primary pathway does not lead to an outcome of its own, and is but a stage in development.

I believe that recognition of two qualitatively distinctive forms of consciousness, each of which uses language and speech differently, opens the way to a different understanding of these ideas and as well sheds light on our understanding of cognitive capabilities in animals. It seems clear that some sort of mentation precedes any expression of language defined as expressive and receptive speech and that the speech development provides a structural template for organizing and expressing this mentation. However, the problem in relating thought and language may be connected to a tendency similar to what I described in the preceding chapter as characteristic of the Chomsky school of linguists, to equate thought with one or the other mental activity; in that case reflective representational thought, and in this one a primary unconscious mind, and hence to overlook the possibility of two conscious mental processes that use language differently. In other words, while those who propose a mental process that cannot be cast into the language of reflective representational thought may be correct, they also fail to recognize the presence of two mental processes each with a separate language expression.

This is an easy mistake to make. Both systems of consciousness use the same formal vocabulary and draw upon the same body of social-cultural knowledge. And once the young child gradually acquires the formal aspects of language – grammar, syntax and morphology – he can use these tools to express either form of consciousness. As primordial consciousness is characterized by belief and certainty rather than relativity and reflection, the person functioning in that mode in an individual-centric culture that privileges reflective representational thought believes he or she is being thoughtful, reasonable and realistic. As primordial consciousness draws upon the same formal body of social and cultural knowledge as reflective representational thought the fact that the meaning is not symbolic may be obscured. This is the same categorical mistake that leads to the conviction that dreams are in essence symbolic because once their imagistic, sensory-perceptual content has been rendered into thoughtful language, the language itself can be interpreted symbolically. In sum, the fundamental semantic differences between the language or primordial consciousness and that of reflective representational thought are not at all apparent to the casual observer.

It is easy to make the related mistaken assumption that because birds and animals seem to employ a meaningful mental process they are capable of thought implicitly defined as recursive self-awareness. Terrestrial placental mammals and birds seem to be able to express themselves in primordial consciousness, with its concrete, stimulus-bound, performative nature, that communicates through pressure and enactment, but only humans are capable of using language as a vehicle of reflection and reference that communicates through language-based interchanges of represented meaning.

Chapter 7

Belief systems and other everyday phenomenology of primordial consciousness and its language

Primordial consciousness and its language undergirds numerous phenomena of everyday life. One of them, psychosis, is manifestly pathological; another, belief systems, is considered normal within some social contexts and pathological in others. Others include altered states of consciousness, and finally, creativity.

Pronouns

To begin with I should like to note a phenomenon of language that seems so ordinary it usually goes unnoticed. That is the use of pronouns in ways that are quite antithetical to their meaning in reflective representational thought. The first-person pronoun "I" has very different meanings when used in the language of representational thought that supports self-awareness, reflection, introspection or recursion, than it has in the language of primordial consciousness, in which it connotes agency; doing or being, but no capacity for recursive reflection about self. Use of the pronoun "I" ordinarily implies that the speaker is a reflective thoughtful person. Similarly, when second and third person pronouns are used in the context of reflective representational thought they imply differentiation of self from other and awareness of another legitimate point of view. Conversely, in the context of belief systems based on primordial conscious mentation, however they make formal differentiation between self and other, in fact they express an undifferentiated belief that the world thinks as the speaker thinks; an identity or state of fusion between self and others. The putative references to others actually animate the world with the person's own mental states. Along with the concrete enactive feature of primordial consciousness this can give speech an imperative, coercive, even intrusive quality. Simple examples are found in political speeches in which the orator assumes a "we believe," or in everyday dining in a restaurant when the wait person, eager to clear the table, says something like "Are we finished?" These semantic differences are often difficult to detect, because both languages utilize the same formal vocabulary and sentence structure, and by definition, in many instances those speaking in the language of primordial consciousness do not "realize" (are not self-aware) that they are doing so.

An interesting example in which the third person pronoun "they" reflects an undifferentiated "I" occurred in an award ceremony on November 27, 2017, commemorating the service of Native American code talkers in WWII. In the course of ostensibly praising these men's heroism President Trump must have associated their ethnicity with his hostile interchanges with Senator Elizabeth Warren, whose ancestry is partly Native American, and whom he has disparagingly referred to on numerous occasions as "Pocahontas." Without any comment bridging the gulf between his praise of the men and his attack on her he stated, "We have a representative in Congress who they say was here a long time ago. They call her Pocahontas. But you know what, I like you."

What is notable is that although this bit of name-calling is original to the president himself, he has contextualized it in the other, using the pronoun "they" twice. His failure to differentiate self and other is further manifest at the conclusion of his statement by confusing the "I" who likes Native Americans with the "they" (objectively "I") who uses "Pocahontas" as an epithet. In classical Freudian theory of unconscious mentation such an utterance would be interpreted as symptomatic; a "Freudian slip" with origins in unconscious or perhaps preconscious conflict related to his hostility towards Warren and perhaps to the Native American minority he is addressing, to be uncovered by free association. Applying the model of two forms of consciousness each with its unique language, however, the use of "they" in a situation rationally calling for the first person "I" suggests the presence of an entirely different form of mental activity, and the transition to an undifferentiated mental state. Further discussion of President Trump's primordial conscious mentation and its language can be found in chapters 10 and 11.

The mental process underlying altered states of consciousness including trance and ecstasy, induced by sleep deprivation, fasting or starvation, self-torture, disciplined meditation and mind-altering drugs, conforms to the characteristics of primordial consciousness. As these are states in which expressive language plays little part, except when they are engaged in as part of a group process, as for example in a mass religious ritual or a rock concert, I will not elaborate them here.

Primordial belief systems

Broadly speaking there are two kinds of belief systems; ones in which we all participate by virtue of our being children of a particular time in history and place within a culture and society, that are a product of a kind of unwitting dogmatism, the result of unavoidable absence of a broader reflective perspective, and others that are not susceptible to reflection and reason even when it is available because they are based on mental activity that is inherently not reflective or recursive. Ludwik Fleck writes about the former:

We walk around without seeing any points, lines, angles, light or shadows, from which we would have to arrange "what is this" by synthesis or reasoning, but we see at once a house, a memorial in a square, a detachment of soldiers, a bookshop window, a group of children, a lady with a dog, all of them ready forms. (...) We look with our own eyes, but we see with the eyes of the collective body, we see the forms whose sense and range of permissible transpositions is created by the collective body. (1947, p. 134)

And, "The individual within the collective is never, or hardly ever, conscious of the prevailing thought style, which almost always exerts an absolutely compulsive force upon his thinking and with which it is not possible to be at variance" (1935, Part II, p. 4). Postmodern theorists including those in disciplines such as cultural anthropology have described the indigenous or contextual nature of many of our ways of looking at ourselves and the world. These are the kinds of belief systems that introduce an irreducible subjectivity into even the most rigorous scientific inquiry, as Thomas Kuhn illustrated when he wrote about paradigm shifts in scientific theories. Psychoanalytic theory is not immune to this problem, as I described in 2011, because its founder reasoned from within the context of what we now think of as the authoritarian and repressive (Oedipal complex) sexist (What do women want? A penis), perspective of 19th century Europe, and more broadly than that, from within the self or individual-centric belief system of Western culture which is very different from the socio-centric perspective of classical Eastern culture and numerous tribal cultures that I describe in chapter 8. Within this contextual limitation, however, minds are still able to function either recursively in reflective representational thought, and can have the flexibility to rely more on one or the other as context and circumstances dictate, as Freud's certainly did. It is the latter kinds of beliefs, based on primordial consciousness and its language and not susceptible to examination when necessary by reflective thought, that are my focus here.

These belief systems are by their nature not amenable to modification by reflective thoughtful logic. Sometimes they border on the delusions characteristic of psychosis. They frequently involve a movement, and the movement usually has a leader – a guru or a priest of a cult, an extreme religion, or the charismatic leader of an extreme reactionary political movement. Belief systems are characterized by affect-driven action; "hunches" or "instincts," and an undifferentiated relationship in which the world is animated by unintegrated aspects of the collective or undifferentiated minds of the leader and participants. The process does not psychologically distinguish external reality, stable consensually agreed-upon facts, logical discrepancies or contradictions. Feeling states, actions and attitudes objectively observable in the subject are attributed to others whose separate reality and characteristics are not appreciated. Language is performative; used concretely as something that has weight and force and functions to induce corresponding emotional states of belief in others, rather than something designed to communicate ideas to be recursively contemplated. The social aspect is contagious and can be observed in the states of frenzy or ecstasy of group participation that are induced. At times such as a religious revival or a rock concert the results may be contained and even constructive, but under other circumstances where the content of primordial conscious mind is concretely driven by unrepresented destructive affects of whose emotional meaning participants are unaware the result can be socially disastrous, and recognized as psychotic, as illustrated in the Manson "family" and on a much larger terrifying scale in some of the phenomena of Hitler's rise to power in Nazi Germany. As John Locke put it, "We should have a great deal fewer disputes in the world if words were taken for what they are, the signs of our ideas only, and not for things themselves" (1714, p. 230).

In the examples that follow I want to make a clear distinction between people who are part of ideological movements and people who have political ideas that fall on different points on the liberal-conservative spectrum, and between religious extremists and others. I want to emphasize another distinction: that having a belief system based upon primordial consciousness in one area of a person's life does not preclude using reflective representational consciousness in other areas. An extreme example is to be found in the history of Nazi Germany. There are many stories of persons who were political fanatics during the day and reasonable loving individuals at night when they came home to their families.

Belief in the findings of science, an external array of experimentally documented facts, is one factor discriminating those functioning in reflective representational consciousness from those functioning exclusively (not optionally and selectively) in primordial consciousness. Many people in the right-wing political and fundamentalist religious communities do not believe the findings of science regarding such things as evolution and global warming. Their internal convictions supersede consensually established external facts and realities and logical causal reasoning. What is here and now is everything, and there is no recursive sense of a sequence of events conforming to principles of logical causality happening over the course of time. As a result such persons conceive of happenings in the world differently than persons functioning from a base of recursive logical representational thought where there are believed to be critical causal sequences. Interpreting extreme climatic events, for instance, a person operating from a religious belief system might cite God's will rather than contemplating a course of events over time and their meaning. Someone motivated by the desire for material gain might feel justified in exploiting natural resources without having to consider future and real consequences. When catastrophic events happen their meaning will be construed not as part of a causal chain but as random acts with no larger meaning, or as the consequence of hostile external forces.

I wish to emphasize once again the difference between liberal and conservative debate couched in the language of reflective representational thought and logic, and disagreement between liberal positions couched in reflective thought and extreme conservative or reactionary positions couched in primordial consciousness. There is neurological evidence in support of the hypothesis that two forms of consciousness have a role in political issues. Kanai, Feilden, Firth and Rees (2011) studied event related potentials (ERP) using MRI in young adults divided into two groups according to political attitudes, liberal and conservative. They found that liberalism tends to be associated with larger gray matter volume in the anterior cingulate cortex and conservativism with a larger right amygdala. Functional studies associate the anterior cingulate cortex with emotion regulation, differentiation, integration, and associated logical reflective thinking and behavior; and the amygdala, part of the limbic system, with emotional intensity and associated belief-driven behavior. It is worthy of note that the amygdala is one of the limbic-paralimbic circuit structures that is also active in dreaming, the quintessential example of primordial consciousness. I return to the subject of political belief systems and their relationship to primordial consciousness in chapters 10 and 11 on language aberration.

Psychosis

Turning to psychosis, Freud (1900a) believed that the primary process is the mental activity that underlies it. Klein's concepts of the paranoid-schizoid position and phantasy elaborate a similar idea. In chapter 3 I derived the concept of primordial consciousness from those seminal beginnings. In 2011 I elaborated how that mental activity is the foundation of psychosis, and explained that it is not the process itself that is abnormal but rather the circumstances and reasons it is used that are socially inappropriate and destructive. This is illustrated in chapter 13, devoted to Caroline and the language of schizophrenia I call "schizophrenese." For now I present a vignette illustrating another common manifestation of primordial consciousness and its language, that I would call a situational psychosis.

I was talking with a friend who works in the mental health field, who had suffered a sudden, life-threatening physical problem about a year before that had required major emergency surgery, a trauma from which she had recovered well physically. When I explained to her the thesis of the book she said she had a story to tell me. After hearing it I asked if she would write it down, and she gave me her permission to include it here.

> When I was about 6 years old my identical twin sister and I were taken to the hospital to have tonsillectomies. It was then common practice not to prepare children for what was about to happen believing that it was better for me not to know about the procedure and the separation from my mother and twin sister. I was told we were going to visit a friend. I could hear her screaming and crying down the hall in another room. I bravely tried to escape my own Hell by trying to reach her to flee the place but was instead apprehended and subsequently tied to my bed, helpless and scared to death.

The following morning I was taken to the operating room, and I have lived with one strong memory of the event: the placement of a mask over my face and the thought that surely I was going to die. I woke to tremendous pain not knowing what had happened to me. It has been a humongous memory to this day with a rise in my blood pressure any time I see a physician unless I have grown to trust her/him. Afterward I suffered what today would be labeled PTSD including a school phobia. I was convinced that someone would "come for me" while I was there.

Before this last surgery I was calm. I had positive experiences with both my surgeon and anesthesiologist who had carefully prepared me for what would happen. The day of surgery I decline any pre-op calming medication having learned that I do well emotionally when I can see and hear and understand [representational thought and language] what is about to happen to me. I even laugh and joke with the surgeon and anesthesiologist. My doctor places a mask over his face and starts to haul out a mask to place on my face. And then I go bonkers! No one had mentioned to me that a mask would be placed on my face when "putting me out." Suddenly I am BACK THERE, and I become another person. I sit up, try to tear the mask out of my surgeon's hand and start yelling, not even trying to control myself. I remember only retrospectively that the surgeon tears off his mask, calls me by name, speaks firmly and loudly to me about how he is going to help me and says words that calm me down. I don't recall exactly what they were. I remember that I enter my familiar world and understand what is about to happen. Later the surgeon says that I became a mad woman and went after him. It was the mask I was trying to destroy.

What I want to emphasize is that I was back there. I experienced a different world of perception. I remember, from the perspective of reflective thought, motor action, all body expression and sensation. In that world I am right THERE. It is all here and now with no sense of time in an undifferentiated present. I just KNOW I am about to die by mask suffocation. Another me merges in an instant, a strong belief that the mask is an instrument of death. It was a protective "do or die." There appear to have been two different senses of being. I remember them both; there has been no melding of them into one integrated experience.

There is not much I can add to her eloquent account. What she calls the "one strong memory of the event" is what I think of as an affect-driven image that is the concrete undifferentiated equivalent of the experience of dying. What is interesting about the way she writes of the presurgical terror experience, which I think of as a situational psychosis induced by the sudden appearance of the mask image, is that the moment she begins to describe the mask being taken out to be placed on her face her language changes from the past tense of memory to the present tense of it happening now. What she describes as a subsequent school phobia is regression from the state of I-thou separateness of reflective representational thought to the state of primordial consciousness when the world is animated in an undifferentiated way with parts of her psyche.

Creativity

Primordial consciousness is the modus operandi of many creative people and underlies many examples of the creative process. I present two examples that have particular relevance to the use of language.

The first is taken from the preface to *The Unlikely Peace at Cuchumaquic* (2012) by Martin Prechtel, an American who grew up in a tribal culture in the Amazon basin and is able to transit between primordial consciousness and reflective symbolic thought in his writings:

> Because of my upbringing inside of languages not containing the objectifying verb "to be" I had a severe allergy to writing "about" things. I felt that when one wrote, the writing itself should be what one wrote. The words were not components of a dead vehicle, but live matter. Language written had to be language that, in its speaking, became, in the manner the words were written, the very thing that would otherwise be written about. One did not write about a horse; one wrote a horse into view, and then as the horse charged off the page into the grassy pastures of the reader's soul, one had to stand back, make room, or be trampled. (2012, p. xv)

The second example is Bob Dylan, who was awarded the 2016 Nobel Prize in literature. Unfortunately copyright laws prevent me from directly quoting the demotic idiom that makes him famous, but the lyrics and poetry I refer to below can be found in chapter 12 of my 2011 book. His primordial conscious functioning is captured in many of his somatic references to wind and breath, which has an ancient connotation of "spirit." In a concrete and certainly not logical interview in the October-November 1962 issue of *Sing Out*, when he was 21 years of age, Dylan explained the song *Blowin' in the Wind* as follows:

> There ain't too much I can say about this song except that the answer is blowing in the wind. It ain't in no book or movie or TV show or discussion group. Man, it's in the wind – and it's blowing in the wind. Too many of these hip people are telling me where the answer is . . .

He is describing a concrete undifferentiated state of psychomotor actualization of which the words and breath are a part; it is what it is, and not a symbol of something else. His playing is fascinating to listen to and watch. With his eyes closed he sings. As his total body syncopates, he blows into his harmonica held by a special attachment next to his mouth, and his hands play acoustic guitar or piano. There seems a sensory-perceptual-psychic-motor identity or actualization with the world about him, and the quality mesmerizes or entrances audiences and tends to induce in them a reciprocal undifferentiated trance state. Friends describe how he intuitively and emotionally absorbed the ambience around him and gave voice or breath to it; as childhood friend Harry Weber says (Shelton, 1987, p. 69), "the way a primitive person might." Weber describes his creative process as an altered drug-like state: "The words seemed to come from somewhere else . . . memory . . . unconscious mind" (p. 70). Many have noted that his voice has taken on distinctly different qualities at different periods of his life, undifferentiated or merged first with Woody Guthrie and subsequently with Johnny Cash, with whom he collaborated many years later. At the beginning of his career he learned about Woody Guthrie and according to his friends and his own recollections almost literally took on his identity, became him. This was a model for the series of identity transformations or mergers later in his life. This is reminiscent of the undifferentiated shape-changing that is characteristic of socio-centric cultures where in a dream life that is considered an aspect of waking reality rather than an altered state people take on the identity of animals or spirits.

Much of what Dylan wrote and sang evokes affective imagery that is not easily decoded as symbolism and seems to have achieved its expressive effect not by communicating ideas in a musical context but by moving his audiences and evoking in them a reciprocal affective-imagistic resonance. He loves to perform in front of audiences, and the performances have the quality of self-induced states of ecstasy. According to Shelton (1985) fellow folk singer Dave van Ronk remarked to Dylan that his song "*A hard rain's a gonna fall*" is "heavy on symbolism" and Dylan is said to have responded "Huh?" In number eight of his *Eleven Outlined Epitaphs* (1963) he writes about rhyming in much the same way that Martin Prechtel wrote about his writing, as a concrete psychomotor process of actualization rather than as a representation; something that is, not a symbol of something else to be decoded. Poem ten of another series of eleven written in the same year is a statement that there is no contradiction, opposites are identical; the question is or contains the answer.

The editor of Robert Shelton's biography of Dylan, Gabrielle Goodchild, commented about Dylan's novel, *The Tarantula*, that it is "a circus of dreams" in which he uses "language of concurrence, coincidence and contradiction," and that "language is pressurized into producing a new and purposeful energy" (Shelton, 1987, p. 236). Shelton himself has this to say:

> The dream-hallucination as mirror of reality: The priest-seer-artist dreams of a reality that lies outside ordinary time and space yet mirrors the everyday world . . . For surrealist artists, dreams, imaginings, even hallucinations, natural or chemical, have helped broaden and deepen the scope of art . . . The artist, as dreamer-in-chief, lends structure, shape, and color to the visions he will, at some point, share with his audience . . . Innumerable Dylan followers have assured me it is *impossible* to understand much of Dylan's 1965–1966 work without dropping acid.

He goes on to liken Dylan's work to that of Blake, Coleridge, Rimbaud and Baudelaire, who "... give existence and substance to that 'other world'" (1987, p. 270). During this period Dylan wrote *Mr. Tambourine Man*, a song that Shelton believes is an expression of Dylan himself:

> ... a sandman for adults, a spirit who draws us out of our daily parade to escape ... playing a song for me, taking me following, casing me under his dancing spell ... Listening to him, we are quite ready to go anywhere. (p. 275) A spiritual journey. In describing *Visions of Johanna*, Shelton quotes Bill King's doctoral thesis (*The Artist in the Marketplace*) that *Tambourine Man* is Dylan's finest poem and that he "... constantly seeks to transcend the physical world to reach the ideal where the visions of Johanna become real" (p. 322). The folk singer Richard Farina made this insightful comment about Dylan's non-recursive mind: "What he says and what he does are the same thing. His expression is precisely what he is ... I don't believe that I understand what is going through his mind." (p. 327)

More examples of the language of primordial consciousness will be found in chapter 10, where I explain that however strange or even bizarre some instances may sound to ears attuned to the "scientific" context of rational reflective symbolic thought, it would be a mistake to equate the language of primordial consciousness with language aberration or with psychosis.

Chapter 8

Primordial consciousness, language, and cultural differences

One of the most important phenomena that the model of two qualitatively different manifestations of consciousness helps to illuminate is a basic difference between socio-centric and individual-centric cultures with regard to how they view the self in relation to the cosmos (Robbins, 1996, 2011). Examples of socio-centric cultures include ethnically homogenous tribal cultures and larger traditional Eastern cultures, particularly Buddhist and Hindu. However, the distinction has increasingly been blurred in recent centuries by the homogenizing impact of Western colonialism. Nowadays the most vivid examples of socio-centric cultures are small tribes that have managed to remain isolated from Western influence, such as the Piraha that Daniel Everett wrote about. My personal experience with the Maori culture of New Zealand, which has with some success resisted colonization by the British, and its use of primordial consciousness, is described elsewhere (2011). Western (European, American) cultures tend to be individual-centric.

From the perspective of individual-centric cultures that value an objectified "reality," rationality, and a "scientific" perspective, the beliefs and actions that characterize socio-centric cultures are often subtly devalued by referring to them as instances of mythology, immaturity, and sometimes even psychosis. My hypothesis from a more relativistic perspective is that the difference has to do with the preference of a particular culture for the kind of reflective thought that characterizes separation in contrast to the mind of collective unity of primordial consciousness. In a collective situation where the mentation and language of primordial consciousness is part of a larger social process the psychological distinctions and differences do not imply cognitive inability to make "realistic" distinctions and act in ways that are functionally adaptive; merely a different way of looking at self and world while so doing.

In this chapter I describe some of the organizing principles of the socio-centric cultures that support primordial consciousness in their members and contrast it with the modal mentation of self-centric culture. Then, taking the Piraha as example of a socio-centric culture I focus on language using the rich descriptions provided by Daniel Everett.

The modal individual centric person has a particular understanding of reality that involves a sense of self separate from others and containing or housing an intrapsychic life. Such an individual reflects on his or her mental content as well as relationship with a separate external world in a logical manner. Science is the pinnacle of this cosmology. Within the relational space the individual person is believed to have a mind that is spatially structured in a horizontally layered hierarchy. The intrapsychic space has two or three subdivisions. In a dualistic model the individual has a thoughtful, rational, conscious part and a mysterious, irrational, less aware part. In the Freudian psychoanalytic model there is a third level of conscience or superego. There are other mental distinctions as well, for example between a remembered or historical past and a present that is very different, between the state of sleep and its unique phenomenon dreaming and the state of wakefulness, and between individual life and its termination.

As I mentioned, the best examples of socio-centric cultures are to be found in small isolated tribes whose essential structure has not been compromised by Western colonization. There is a similarity among them with regard to how they view person and cosmos that is remarkable considering that so many of them are separated, existentially in terms of geography and communication, and over the millennia as well (Eliade, 1964; Nicholson, 1987). These cultures are socio-centric or collective in so far as they do not differentiate a self requiring introspection that is separate from the cosmos (Robbins, 1996). Their spatial divisions are analogous to those of individual-centric cultures but the distinctions are within the self-object undifferentiated cosmos rather than the individual mind. They include dualistic and tripartite distinctions related to such matters as good and evil; the ancestral world and the current world of the living; the soul or spirit and the body; the underworld, the earth and the sky. Ancestors are every bit as alive as existing members of one's family.

In sociocentric cultures, dreaming is just as real and reasonable as any other "reality" (Fabrega & Silver, 1970; Kracke, 1999; Nakashima-Degarrod, 1989; Vitebsky, 2001; and others summarized by Walter & Fridman, 2004). The dream is believed to involve not a movement between waking and sleep but a time or space travel of the soul or spirit to another place or supernatural dimension or even to a self that has been changed, for example into another person or animal. Such experiences are looked upon as ominous or portentous encounters rather than as informative about unconscious aspects of individual mind. The soul or spirit is not believed to be isomorphic with the body, but rather an essence that can travel in time and space. What persons from individual-centric cultures call death or termination of individual life is for socio-centric cultures the permanent severance of the relationship between the soul and body. Comprehension and action is based on undifferentiated sensory-perceptual animation of the cosmos by affect driven states. These states are analogous to dreaming in Western cultures but members of tribal cultures do not make qualitative distinctions between waking life and the state of dreaming. Spiritual cultures are generally led by shamans or priests, whose functions are analogous to some combination of those of the executive, judicial and legislative aspects of government, and respected scientists, in individual-centric cultures. The shaman is the expert in experiencing and interpreting the significance of phenomena; someone who "sees" and experiences things that do not fit into familiar categories, for example combinations of animal and human, one sex and the other. Nicholson writes that "... the shaman comes to know ultimate undifferentiated reality through his ecstatic experience and to know cultural differentiation through his analytic ability; further, he understands the need to arrange the world. Now he gathers this knowledge and goes to work" (p. 69).

To illustrate the relationship between the role of primordial consciousness in the mental activity characteristic of socio-centric cultures and its language, I summarize observations about the Piraha culture made by Daniel Everett (2005, 2008) based on his unusual experience and knowledge both as cultural anthropologist and linguist.

Everett's general conclusion is that "Piraha culture constrains communication to concrete here and now subjects which fall within the immediate experience of interlocutors" (2005, p. 621). He calls this the *immediacy of experience principle* (2008). The Piraha live entirely in the present moment in which reality is synonymous with immediate sensory-perceptual-motor experience. If something or someone is out of sight it is absent from discourse until once again concretely present. When present again the subject is familiar but as there is no constant mental representation the experience that comprises relevant past to a Westerner is not remembered. Piraha language expresses what *is* and not what *was* or *will be* or what might be food for (recursive) thought, so to speak. It is not used symbolically to represent other things or abstract ideas.

Despite having no internal mental map or symbolic representation the Piraha have no trouble navigating through life, which should not be surprising despite the Western tendency to equate the mental process described with irrationality, unreality, delusion and the like, as the primordial conscious mentation has to do with how things are understood and responded to, and is separate from the capacity for accurate or even skilled perceptual-motor function which may be sharper, or at least is different from that of Westerners as these people live and survive in nature without the aid of technology. Places are identified by concrete associations to things like the personal activity that is or was done there, or an identifying geographical feature or a connection with particular wildlife. Directions are given not in abstract concepts (right, left) but in relation to similarly immediately palpable concrete aspects of the environment and physical being.

In this world of immediacy there is no concept of time; no words to express past, future or duration; no verbalized sense of logical sequence, causality or consequences, although as I have suggested, there is a different kind of logic that is operative. It follows that there is no memory in the sense of something that happened another time and no collective history: all aspects suggestive of absence of recursion. Piraha can recount experiences within the sensory-perceptual lifetime of the person, but they are told as though they are happening currently.

They do not anticipate or plan for what Westerners conceptualize as future, either. For example they do not stockpile goods and supplies.

As their experience is immediate so their discourse contains nothing a Westerner could label fantasy in the sense of thoughtful reverie, or shared cultural fiction or mythology. Piraha mental activity seems devoid of the as-if qualities of abstraction, symbolization and related logic that characterize thought. These people do not make art, tell stories that involve imagination or fantasy, or create myths. This literal quality, lacking symbolism or analogy, was illustrated when a visitor attempted to communicate why he was spraying himself with bug repellent by imitating with gesture and sound the sound and flight of the insects and the activity of killing them, hoping that his pantomime would elicit thought and a representational name. He concluded with a gesture with recursive implications, slapping an imaginary mosquito. The Piraha who were observing the show turned to Everett in puzzlement and asked why the man was hitting himself. Yet they do have a "living" cosmology, as exemplified for Everett when he was awakened early one morning by the excited cries of the villagers, who were massed on the river bank and pointing to their God who was visible to all of them (but not to Everett and his family) on the far bank.

It is not surprising that the Piraha have no written language, something that would require a degree of abstraction and mental representation. And their spoken language lacks abstract qualitative descriptors. For example, while the natives are sensitive and responsive to color cues they do not have abstract words for colors. Instead they substitute likeness or identity. The object is not "red," it is like blood. They do not remember the name of a visitor; instead he or she is dubbed by the name of a native Piraha whose features bear some resemblance. Their language has few pronouns; instead they refer to concrete and specific names.

What Westerners might think about as ideas, to the Piraha are things placed adjacent to one another, sequenced by contiguity or linearity rather than by temporal or causal logic. There are no subordinate clauses in Piraha speech, no recursive combining of one idea within another in a sentence.

Piraha language contains few kinship terms, and kinship bonds such as marriage are loosely maintained and very much of the moment. The most likely explanation is that they do not have abstract ideas of connection or bonding or an enduring representation of the relevant emotions. Someone who is gone from immediate sight or hearing is no longer a subject of discourse, although he or she is readily recognized on return. While the Piraha show affect and are generally a playful people who help one another out in practical matters, they do not seem to be aware of feelings about one another in the sense of enduring representations or emotional states that are necessary for more abstract notions of attachment. Where feelings of anger might be expectable there is instead action or enactment, usually in the form of distance, disengagement, or distraction from the relationship.

Everett recounts vivid experiences about how Piraha deal with death and child rearing that are also consistent with the mentation of primordial consciousness.

These include examples of the absence of emotional representation, of a sense of time past and future, and of actions and consequences. A woman died a protracted death in breach childbirth while observers seemed indifferent, presumably lacking in the ability to foresee consequences. Everett recorded subsequent dialogue with her husband who repeated over and over words like "she is not here now" accompanied by tone and behavior that conveyed his obvious distress, but devoid of any articulation of emotion or attachment.

Infants and small children are given what to Western eyes is an unusual degree of "freedom" to do whatever they want. Everett notes the absence of punishment for forbidden behavior or protection from harm, both of which involve a sense of time and ability to think logically about consequences. He observed a scene where an infant played with a sharp knife, risking self-mutilation, in the presence of seemingly unconcerned adults. Infants are nursed until the arrival of another child, often around four years, and then weaned abruptly and totally, often screaming for nights on end while parents, nursing the new baby, seem oblivious. Ordinary Western conclusions about such behaviors, for example that the Piraha do not care about one another, are belied by their close community, affectionate and helping attitudes toward one another. During the first three years of life there is a very close physical and emotional sharing bond between parents and infants. As adults they are a tightly bound social community of individuals who share similar experiences and similar basic affect states. This is strongly suggestive of positive primary attachment experience and sharing of primordial consciousness.

While the fact that the Piraha have no mythology about such things as creation and destruction might suggest that Piraha is not a spiritual culture; the spirituality is enacted in a concrete undifferentiated way in such beliefs that they can change shape and identity and become spirits. They share a belief in a spirit or dream world that they "see," and collectively interact with, although they do not "think about." They share a sensory-perceptual-motor cosmology that for them is simply another aspect of reality. Their attitude toward dreams is that they are another kind of immediate real experience. Behavior that to the Western observer seems to involve supernatural mythological beliefs and practices is real, not symbolic or fantastic. The spirit or dream world is equivalent in reality value to what we think of as the "real" world, and is contacted through spirit transit into the land of the dead, often in enactments where persons are believed to change form and function. In the prologue to his book Everett (2008) recounts being present at what appeared to him and his family to be a mass hallucination by villagers, of Xigagai, an evil spirit. A large group of natives could "see" Xigagai clearly and describe him in detail, and they were amazed that Everett could not.

The Piraha exemplify a culture that uses primordial consciousness in a way that is adaptive and contextually normal. In a broader sense they exemplify the fact that entire cultures may be based on primordial consciousness rather than reflective symbolic thought, and that "inability" to appreciate reality in a Western thoughtful sense in no way implies the inability to appreciate and cope with reality in a cognitive-adaptive sense.

The existence of cultures whose language lacks recursion proves that Chomsky's belief that all languages must conform to the principle of recursion is incorrect and affirms the necessity of a theoretical model of two distinctive conscious mental processes and their language. While the evidence suggests that social factors play an important role in language formation it does not disprove Chomsky's contention that language itself – defined more broadly and dualistically than he did – has an underlying neurological template.

Chapter 9

Emergence of the bilingual sense of self during the attachment phase

The bilingual self develops, beginning with the emergence of primordial consciousness within the undifferentiated matrix of the mother-infant relationship, and leads to the later gradual emergence of reflective representational thought, a process that is not finished until the completion of mental maturation during adolescence. The process begins with mother-infant attachment, either in the form of secure and predictable attachment or desperate insecure entanglement as a consequence of some combination of maternal rejection, hostility and invalidation.

Our ideas about attachment and its importance can be traced back to Bowlby and his classic three volume series (1969), although there are many other important contributions including Klein and those influenced by her as summarized in chapter 3, Piaget (1936), Spitz (1957), Fraiberg (1959), Mahler (Mahler, Pine, & Bergman, 1975), Stern (1985), and others too numerous to mention here. Bowlby wrote that attachment communication includes "facial expression, posture, and tone of voice" (1969, p. 120). Two years later, inspired by his work, the Robertson couple, James and Joyce, made a now classical film series showing the nuanced subtle interactions of gesture, facial expression and sound between infants and their mothers during stages of attachment, separation and reunion (1971). Since then, and with the emergence of sophisticated neuroscience technology such as fMRI, research into infant-mother attachment and the emergence of self and language has exploded. Patricia Kuhl (2010) summarized research using noninvasive functional brain measurement techniques such as fMRI and measurement of ERP (event related potentials) that can safely be applied even to newborn infants.

On the infant side of the ledger, the first language emerges from a matrix including the neural capacity for primordial consciousness signified by REM sleep, the coming online of the auditory system, and the crucial catalytic force of the maternal voice. Somewhere around the end of the second trimester of fetal life, the auditory system, our first functional sensory capacity, comes online. This is approximately the same time that REM activity is detectable, suggesting both the capacity for dreaming, and the emergence of primordial consciousness. The fetus awakens, so to speak, and enters the mental-social world of being through interaction with maternal sounds, including heartbeat, intestinal and respiratory noises, and of most importance to this discussion, the musical prosody of mother's voice as she talks to her unborn child as well as to others, using language and other forms of vocalization.

On the maternal side, mothers reflexively begin to interact with their infants by the last trimester of pregnancy when the manifestations of quickening or movement unrelated to maternal volition provides inescapable evidence of a new and separate life within. At first mothers use the music of their voices; spoken words and sounds to communicate with this new presence. After birth their repertory expands to include gestures and facial expressions as well. In chapter 4 I described the "mother tongue," also known as motherese or IDL (infant directed language), which is the language of primordial consciousness that parents, especially and for the purposes of this discussion mothers, reflexively engage in with their infants. Recent neurological studies of the primordial motherese interaction between mothers and infants have focused on what are called mirror systems (Kuhl & Meltzoff, 1996; Meltzoff & Decety, 2003; Pulvermuller, 2005; Rizzolatti, 2005; Rizzolatti & Craighero, 2004).

Intrauterine responses to mother's voice are described by Condon and Sander (1974). At birth the infant recognizes mother's voice and prefers it to others (Kolata, 1984; Mehler & Christophe, 2000). "The melodies of mother's speech are compelling auditory stimuli, which are particularly effective in eliciting emotion in pre-verbal infants" (Fernald, 1996, p. 71). Meissner remarks on the similarity of the affect-laden prosody of human speech, especially between mother and infant, to singing (2008, p. 36). In chapter 8 I noted that Everett's (2005, 2008) description of the singular language of the Piraha, which fits the description of a shared primordial consciousness, as having a whistling quality. Newborn infants can distinguish mother's voice from a stranger's voice from a single syllable in the first second of speech (Moon, Randall, Zernzach, & Kuhl, 2015). Fernald (1993, 1996) described universal prosodic patterns used by mothers in affective dialogue including falling pitch to soothe, rising pitch to gain the baby's attention, and alternating pitch to maintain attention. Mothers also modify their prosody to regulate the child's arousal and attention. Infants respond to the mother tongue of the caregiver by gradually developing the musicality or prosody that will later accompany their own phrases and sentences, and babble in sentence-like musicality long before the time during the first or second year when they acquire the actual words and syntax to accompany the music.

Contrary to the belief of linguists including Chomsky and Pinker, studies suggest that the development of the language of primordial consciousness *in utero* includes not only the learning of prosody but also of actual words and sentences within the self-other undifferentiated system of consciousness that prevails at that time. Kolata (1984) concluded that infants who were read Doctor Seuss's "Cat in a Hat" twice a day beginning in the last six weeks of gestation sucked preferentially after birth when mother read that story in contrast to when she read another one. Partanen et al. (2013) repeatedly exposed fetuses during the last trimester to particular nonsense combinations of syllables and discovered that as infants they recognized and preferentially responded to them in contrast to others.

There is evidence that the mother tongue is not simply a vehicle for the gradual linear development of reflective representational thought and language but is part of the development of separate mental process, primordial consciousness, and its language. Reflective representational thought does not develop until later infancy and childhood as the brain matures. Studies of children adopted by parents who speak different languages than that of the birth mother reveal that the phonemes and prosody of language of the birth mother during the last trimester and in the first year and a half of life are part of a unique form of learned language. Learning through prosody and presumably primordial consciousness peaks somewhere between 3 months and 1 year of age and then gradually declines, and by age 5–7 ceases (Best & McRoberts, 2003; Rivera-Gaxiola, Silvia-Pereyra & Kuhl, 2005; Tsao, Liu & Kuhl, 2006; Werker & Tees, 1984). Even if the child is adopted into a family that speaks a very different language the language that was learned then is only dormant, and the infant can subsequently learn the mother's language more quickly than another child, and with appropriate accent (Choi, Cutler & Broersma, 2017). This is why children who have been exposed to foreign languages during the first few months of life learn those languages much more rapidly and with appropriate prosody or accent later in life than those who have not had such exposure, and why, sometime around ages 5–7 it is no longer possible to learn a foreign language with its native accent. It can be inferred that there is a distinction between the primordial mother tongue language and the language of reflective representational thought, and even into adult life the content learned in primordial consciousness has unique power to facilitate subsequent acquisition of language.

Prominent though sound – prosody – is in the production of the mother tongue, it does not appear to be an essential component of the language of motherese. Masataka (1998) studied a group of deaf mothers and their congenitally deaf infants and discovered unique qualities of motherese in sign language – slower tempo, exaggerated gesture, and more repetition – and demonstrated that the infants responded preferentially to a tape of their mothers signing material in motherese than when the same material was presented by other adults. The fact that after approximately age 5 children are much slower learning sign language, a finding analogous to the age limits learning a language with native accent, is further evidence of the language difference between the mother tongue and reflective thought.

The language presumably associated at least in part with reflective representational thought begins to develop between 18 and 36 months of age (Johnson & Newport, 1989). The frontal lobes and myelination, the substrate of reflective symbolic thought, gradually emerge over the course of many years. The language of reflective symbolic thought, is in a sense a second language. At the same time that it begins to emerge, in the latter half of the first year, the unique learning associated with the mother tongue gradually recedes into the social background, used less and less, so that by ages 5–7 it is no longer possible to learn a second language with its mother tongue prosody or accent. Interestingly, that is the age of the first concrete separation from the family and the commencement of formal education in many cultures. The reason may be that primordial consciousness and its language is the mental activity of the solipsistic undifferentiated self, prior to separation. But as I described in earlier chapters, primordial consciousness and its mental activity does not cease, but continues under selected circumstances, dreaming being the most obvious example, into adult life.

What about speech? Speech production centers in the inferior frontal cortex and Broca's area do not respond to spoken verbal stimuli at birth whereas auditory areas do. Speech areas come on line after 3 months (Imada et al., 2006). D'Odorico & Jacob (2006) studied a group of late-talking infants and found that their mothers tended to interact with them vocally using lower and flatter pitch.

According to McNeill (1970) the capacity for grammatical speech emerges around 1½ years of age and is complete by 3½. Primitive phonemes appear toward the end of the first year (Glucksberg & Danks, 1975). Prior to the ability to form recognizable sentences expressive babbling or stringing together sounds with sentence-like prosody or intonation emerge (Church, 1966). According to Lenneberg (1967) crying generally precedes cooing, then musical babbling, followed by holophrastic speech in which single words seem to imply entire propositions or ideas, and finally by the emergence of syntactic structures typical of the particular language. In the second half of the first year, the child begins to concretely integrate action, sound and facial expression in order to express wants to caregivers. A bit later the receptive component emerges and the infant begins to respond to simple questions and requests expressed in similar somatic-motoric ways. All these operations are preverbal in the sense of equating language with speech, but indicate the degree to which language is present and being processed. The child is mentally active, integrating receptive and expressive components, and can comprehend and respond to the language of others before he or she acquires the use of language in the form of speech. Erreich (2003) remarks: ". . . infants' comprehension of spoken language precedes their language production, leading to the conclusion that infants under the age of 12 months have mental representations for linguistic elements" (p. 556). I believe that these are not constant stable representations but evanescent images consistent with the mental activity of primordial consciousness and that the language of reflective representational symbolic thought, containing recursion is truly a second language that develops later.

The social and cultural context in which mother and infant interact plays a crucial role in determining the meaning of these earliest interactions, and this aspect of development is critical to the questions explored in subsequent chapters about the content of primordial consciousness and its relationship to adult language, ordinary or aberrant. Fonagy and Target (1997) point out that (at least in individual-centric cultures) mother approaches the infant with a question in mind: What does the infant want?, and that the question reflects both the mother's idiosyncratic personality and agenda and contemporary cultural stereotypes about infancy. In socio-centric cultures, for example among the Beng in West Africa, infant cries are viewed as expressions of the language of dead ancestors whose souls the babies embody. The mother's task is to decipher what the baby/ancestor wants her to do (Gottlieb, 2004). This is not totally different from the situation in some Western cultural groups in which the infant is felt by parents to reincarnate characteristics of deceased family members (ancestors). Mothers in all cultures rely on "experts" on the wisdom of the contemporary culture of child-rearing for help in figuring out "What does my baby want from me?" and "What should I be doing?" Litowitz (2009, 2011) comments how words and language are formed out of the context of maternal and cultural beliefs and expectations, which are then transmitted to the child. She remarks about the undifferentiated nature of language in early development that it is never completely clear whose desire is being expressed; mother's, infant's or that of the collective culture. Mother uses her knowledge to establish a shared sense of reality (Rommetveit, 1974) which the baby can express and elaborate with his available vocabulary (e.g., facial expression, postures, crying, fussing). The baby now has a growing body of content with which to receive and express the language of primordial consciousness.

Self-reference in speech is a first step in development of reflection and recursion. According to Sharpless (1985), first person pronouns that appear in speech prior to about 19–22 months tend to be stereotypic, by which she means concrete and contextual rather than truly representational. Second person pronoun use is very limited and probably still reflects the primordial conscious state of fusion or undifferentiation between self and other. In other words, the first "I" involves awareness of being and of agency or action, but not that the bearer is a self with an internal mind.

At about 23–25 months children begin to appreciate that they have a self, and the process of reflective representational consciousness commences, including introspection or recursion. With this development "I" can express subjective awareness, and reciprocally the use of second and third person pronouns develops as a way of denoting social roles in conversation. The child begins to refer to his or her activities and to inner affective states (Greenspan & Shanker, 2005). Around this time the capacity to recognize self in the mirror develops. Some children continue to use a third person designation in referring to themselves for a considerable period (Church, 1966). Galatzer-Levy & Cohler remark how "mine" announces the idea of possession and ownership with its special entitlement. "In the first part of the third year children become increasingly self-descriptive. Earlier the child mostly talks about the environment, labeling objects and describing activities. Now the child begins to spontaneously comment on her own activities" (1993, pp. 68–69). Along with growing self and social contextual awareness there is a transition from the primordial conscious language of agency, being and doing in the world, to the language of reflective representational thought and related awareness of the differentiated other, as manifest by the "show and tell" that is such an important aspect of early development.

Labeling of one's body parts also begins around this time. Fraiberg (1959) notes that these developments coincide with the Piagetian transition from sensorimotor thinking to development of object permanence and adds, "The constitution of a self is the subjective correlate of the constitution of objects" (p. 170). These developments in the period approximately between the second and third year signify the commencement of development of reflective thought characterized by continuous mental representations. As we shall see in chapter 11 on the pathology of early attachment, this is not a transition all children are able to make, although the continued acquisition of formal language that is common to both mental processes may effectively masquerade this fact. It is important to realize that even when the transition is made in the process of a normal developmental trajectory, the capacity for and use of primordial conscious mentation and its language persists; it simply becomes regulated by self-awareness and self-reflection in the context of what is and is not socially appropriate.

Popper remarks on the normal development of differentiation and the awareness of otherness:

> The rudiments of the naming process play a significant role in that he becomes able to recognize, distinguish, and name objects ... All this is deeply affected by the acquisition of speech; especially when the child becomes conscious of his name, and when he learns to name the various parts of his body, and, most important, when he learns to use personal pronouns. (Popper & Eccles, 1985, p. 49)

It is important to recognize the limitations of these studies, and not to fall into the trap of confusing formal and functional proficiency with language with the content it expresses and its psychological meaning. These studies by and large objectify and record the formal learning of distinctions between aspects of one's body and between oneself and another person but the formal aspects and the meaning may not be consistent.

This time of pronoun change must in normal development be a watershed signifying movement toward reflective representational thought, bringing with it self-object differentiation, development of constant rather than unintegrated concrete, stimulus bound imagery, and the ability to begin separating from the primary caregiver; the emergence from a concrete stimulus-bound enactive mental process, and the opportunity to develop a separate reflective self. However, both developments emerge from the matrix of attachment, normal or disturbed, with mother and her mind with its combination of social-cultural imbeddedness and personal idiosyncrasy. Jacques remarks that:

> A voice does not express only one individual. Speech does not originate solely in the self, nor in the other. A voice that belonged absolutely to one

person could never make itself understood. And if it is true that my original condition is to be in a relation, and that language is specifically a mode of verbal interaction, a medium of joint actions and semantic transactions which brings at least two parties into play, then there can never be, at least in any nontrivial sense, such a thing as a private voice. (1991, p. 277)

The use of language as we ordinarily think of it develops from an attachment matrix in which it did not exist; a preexisting mental process. Damasio writes:

The idea that self and consciousness would emerge *after* language, and would be a direct construction of language, is not likely to be correct. If self and consciousness were born de novo from language, they would constitute the sole instance of words without an underlying concept. (1999, pp. 107–108)

Language develops from the interaction of genetic unfolding of the infant's innate potential with the primordial consciousness expressions of the mothering person during the undifferentiated attachment phase and the early years subsequent to it. Under the best of circumstances language development is an incredibly complex process involving learning the mother tongue of undifferentiation and using it to learn the formal structure of the language into which the speaker is born, and subsequently and gradually, learning reflective representational thought, the language of separation, and the different way in which formal language expresses it. But the "normal" attachment process assumed in the research studies I have cited cannot be taken for granted. The next chapters illustrate instances of primordial conscious language and the complexity of determining whether they are aberrant, and the kinds of problems that can arise during the attachment phase that are determinative of language aberration.

Chapter 10

What characterizes language aberration?

I have outlined the normal development of attachment and language, first through primordial consciousness and then through the gradual acquisition of reflective representational consciousness. How can this process go awry and what are some of the consequences?

What is it that characterizes aberrant language? What distinguishes it from language that is simply unusual, remarkable, arresting, creative, uncultured or offensive? Primordial consciousness plays an important role in language aberration yet paradoxically it is of itself normal. What part does the idiosyncratic meaning of words and phrases in the language of primordial consciousness learned as part of a pathological attachment process play in language aberration? And what about the role of contemporary interpersonal, social and cultural context with its implicit expectations about the mix of the language of primordial consciousness and reflective, symbolic thought? For example, those who attend a Bob Dylan concert have a way of listening and a set of expectations that are different from those attending a scientific conference. And the kind of interaction in a political gathering is qualitatively different depending on whether the speaker is mobilizing an emotional rally or trying to create an intellectual alliance. And finally, what is the relationship, if any, between language aberration and determination of mental illness or normality?

What follows is based on the assumption that beneath the differences in the formal languages of the world exist fundamental similarities having to do with the two basic languages of all humans, that of primordial consciousness and reflective representational thought. As an English speaking clinician and writer I am assuming that the language aberrations I observe in working with my patients have analogous expression in persons who speak other national languages.

The aberrations I illustrate are often not readily apparent to the ordinary observer. The clinical examples of speech aberration I present in subsequent chapters, with the possible exception of Caroline, who had been diagnosed schizophrenic, come from persons whose speech and writing would appear to most observers under ordinary circumstances entirely normal, and whose aberrant aspects emerged only in the intensive situation of the particular intimate relationship known as psychoanalytic therapy.

And to further confuse matters, some of the most bizarre examples of speech, as I illustrate with quotations from Caroline in chapter 13, actually conform to the formal principles of language regarding vocabulary, grammar and syntax, and morphology. With regard to morphology, strange as the neologisms characteristic of schizophrenic persons may sound, the rules or processes by which they are formed (such as the use of basic affixes, compounding, onomatopoeia, proper noun transformation, clipping and blending) seem identical to those used in forming perfectly acceptable words. In fact, neologisms, among the strangest manifest features of language, are not necessarily examples of aberrant language, for they are hardly exclusive to schizophrenia. If we study how language evolves over time through successive iterations of dictionaries, many ultimately respectable and widely used words begin life as neologisms. The distinction is that the motivation for forming some neologisms, especially in schizophrenia, may be solipsistic and noncommunicative whereas the neologisms that eventually become common parlance reflect creative efforts to expand the scope of language and social communication.

The political divide between more liberal elements who tend to be individual-centric and (not always) to use the language of reflective representational thought, and more extreme conservative elements whose language is expressive of primordial consciousness is a fertile field for examples of the difficulty deciding whether language is aberrant. In the preface to his book *The Liberal Imagination* Lionel Trilling writes about political divisions and describes a process that sounds like primordial consciousness: "The conservative impulse and reactionary impulse do not, with some isolated and some ecclesiastical exceptions, express themselves in ideas but only in action or in irritable mental gestures which seek to resemble ideas" (1964, p. ix). The word "irritable" relates, I believe to the content, but the rest of Trilling's comment might be a description of the excerpts I am about to present although I substitute conservative for reactionary.

Here is a sentence from a speech given by Sarah Palin, former governor of Alaska, to rouse an audience during the presidential primary campaign of Donald Trump early in 2016. Strange as it seems, can it be called aberrant? "Well then, funny, ha-ha, not funny, but now what they're doing is wailing, 'Well, Trump and his trumpeters, they're not conservative enough'" (*New York Times*, January 20, 2016). The internally contradictory, affect-driven, imagistic, undifferentiated quality is evident, reflective of primordial consciousness. Commentators generally found the speech illogical but it succeeded in exciting the audience, most of whom so far as subsequent interviews revealed, seemed to believe it was within normal limits, promoting the cause of her candidate. Whether the language is aberrant depends on the "eye" (language) of the beholder as dictated by the expectations of the particular context or social situation.

The presidential campaign, and as of this writing the tumultuous presidency of Donald Trump, provides another remarkable example of mental activity and associated language of primordial consciousness that highlights the difficulty of determining when language is aberrant. The president is typically portrayed in the process of oratory, with wide open mouth, finger pointing at his audience, gesturing as he speaks. His narrative is affect-driven, self-referential, tending toward grand pronouncements and attacks on his enemies. He proudly asserts that he functions on what he calls instinct, and that he is always right. He seems unable to maintain a logically coherent or recursively reflective train of thought for any significant period of time without inconsistency and contradiction. Without any evidence of thoughtful reflective restraint he impulsively discharges affectively loaded words as concrete things in his "tweets." They often take the form of attacks on others, and contain beliefs not substantiated by and even at odds with commonly accepted facts, as I elaborate below. In these attacks he does not seem to differentiate aspects of self from other in that he attacks views and actions he misperceives or exaggerates in others while engaging in them without awareness himself. This process of misattribution is what Klein calls projective identification, the difference between her view and mine being that she conceives of it as a secondary defensive activity whereas I conceive of it as contextually inappropriate use of primordial consciousness. The absence of self-object differentiation is also manifest in his intolerance of separateness in others who venture to think, believe or act in a manner different from him; his demand for "loyalty" in the sense of agreement with him rather than allegiance to a larger external reality or law, and his efforts to coerce or eliminate those who do not agree with him.

His words have no fixed meaning in so far as he is inconsistent and self-contradictory; they do not designate an internally representationally constant or objectively constant external reality so much as they do his evanescent affectively shifting inner imagistic states. And they are often at odds with his actions. In this world of belief, as in the dream, there is no such thing as a stable internal mental representation and hence external, verifiable fact, or a prior statement to be reflected on and honored. When confronted with what he has said or done that takes into account objective reality and documented facts, he often claims he never said the words or did the actions in question, and characterizes those who quoted them as liars or purveyors of "fake news." He changes his views regularly without recognition that he has contradicted himself. Trump has gone so far as to assert that he does not believe some of the consensually agreed upon findings of science, the findings of government agencies that have conducted detailed investigations, photographic evidence of things like crowd size, or the former president's legitimate citizenship, and he has asserted that he possesses facts to the contrary, which, however, are no more than beliefs in so far as they are never divulged. His agent, Kellyanne Conway, referred to this as "alternative facts." It should be noted that there is no reason to doubt the accuracy of his sensory-perceptual apparatus; what is at stake is how his mind processes and interprets things. The *New York Times* has compiled transcripts of some of his statements that exemplify what I have described. PolitiFact, an organization with a website devoted to checking the factual accuracy of statements made by politicians, has compiled a long list of his erroneous and contradictory claims.

Here is an example of Trump's self-contradiction. On April 8, 2017, the *New York Times* editorial board reported on his response to a question they asked about the effectiveness of the wall he proposed to build between the USA and Mexico. His response: "By the way, if you want to know if a wall works, just ask Israel. Israel built a wall and it works." The editorial board pointed out to him that it was not working and he responded "Yeah, I know. Well no. Now they're doing the rockets, yeah. That's a – they have a – different – they probably have a bigger – they have a different kind of a problem. You have to build a real wall. They don't have a real wall now. They don't have a wall that works."

Shear (2017) summarized an interview with President Trump, from which I quote, by *Time Magazine* Washington Bureau Chief Michael Scherer. Regardless of what external fact or reality or whatever internal contradiction or reversal he is confronted with that would lead a person operating in reflective representational thought to acknowledge error or incorrectness, Trump repeatedly counters with the belief that it is the people who say he is wrong who are wrong, and he is always right. He says he is guided by gut feelings. "What am I going to tell you? I tend to be right. I'm an instinctual person, I happen to be a person that knows how life works." Utterances from other sources, no matter how unsubstantiated or fantastic, are true if they echo his rightness, and the media from which he gets them are in his mind of the moment respectable, but if a media source disagrees it is called "fake news" or a media conspiracy against him, even if it is one he previously relied on as the source of some of his beliefs. "I turn on the TV, open the newspapers, and I see stories of chaos. Chaos! Yet it is the exact opposite." Scherer repeatedly questions Trump about tweeting that former President Obama had him wiretapped, without any evidence other than unsubstantiated claims made by several people that he read in the media, and despite the fact that the head of the FBI and the Justice Department said there was no evidence whatsoever to support the claim. Trump replies in various ways:

> Now remember this. When I said wiretapping, it was in quotes. Because a wiretapping is, you know today it is different than wire tapping. It is just a good description. But wiretapping was in quotes ... I have, look. I have articles saying it happened. But you have to take a look at what they, they just went out at a news conference. Devin Nunes had a news conference. I mean I don't know, I was unable to see it, because I am at meetings, but they just had a news conference talking about surveillance. Now again, it is in quotes. That means surveillance and various other things.

Of his sources of the unsubstantiated claims he says: "I have a lot of respect for Judge Napolitano, and he said that three sources have told him things that would make me right ... I'm quoting highly respectable people from highly respected television networks." Now the media are respectable. He goes on to say: "I don't know where these wiretaps came from. They came from someplace.

That is what they should find out." And suddenly the response shifts, and the sources of leakage of private and even classified information that during the presidential campaign he applauded as they exposed problems in his opponent, even urging the Russian president, if he was behind it, to do more, now become the enemy:

> And you know the real story here is about the leakers. OK? You don't write about that. But the real story here is, who released General Flynn's name? Who released, who released my conversations with Australia, and who released my conversation with Mexico? To me, Michael, that's the story, these leakers, they are disgusting. These are horrible people.

Scherer points out to him that the government intelligence community has said there is no evidence to support his claims: "You are saying to me now, that you don't believe the intelligence community when they say your tweet was wrong," and Trump replies:

> I'm not saying – no, I'm not blaming. First of all, I put Mike Pompeo in. I put Senator Dan Coats in. These are great people. I think they are great people and they are going to, I have a lot of confidence in them. So hopefully things will straighten out. But I inherited a mess.

Scherer asks President Trump about the fact that in the course of discussing the threat of terrorism in the world he said a terrible thing had happened in Sweden the previous day when in fact nothing had happened. "I talked about Sweden, and may have been somewhat different, but the following day, two days later, they had a massive riot in Sweden, exactly what I was talking about, I was right about that." Once again Scherer comments on Trump's lack of a reflective awareness of time, and asks if it is not important to know which day it was, and what went before and what after, and Trump replies, "No I am saying I was right." Trump concludes the interview by saying, "I can't be doing so badly, because I'm president, and you're not. You know. Say hello to everybody, OK?"

Trump "speaks" in the language of primordial consciousness. But that is not sufficient to call his language pathological, as some mental health professionals, even among my psychoanalytic colleagues, have done. I think it is important to distinguish psychopathology from language aberration and both from language that, however strange, is acceptable within contextual boundaries. In chapter 3 I described the confusion between phenomena based on primordial consciousness that are normal, however unusual they may seem, and those that are labeled pathological. The problem originated with Freud's confusion about whether primary process phenomena are normal, pathological, or somehow both, and was perpetuated by Klein's description of similar phenomenology using the concepts of the paranoid schizoid position and phantasy. Freud believed the primary process, which I have traced as the forerunner of the concept of primordial consciousness, is the underpinning of schizophrenia. He believed that it is inherently psychotic in the sense of creating a subjectively wishful view of the world that he labeled hallucinatory and delusional. He wrote that "A dream, then, is a psychosis with all the absurdities, delusions and illusions of a psychosis . . ." (1940e, p. 172). In 1915 he wrote, "In schizophrenia *words* are subjected to the same process as that which makes the dream-images out of latent dream-thoughts – to what we have called the primary psychical process" (1915e, p. 198). Freud did not try to reconcile how and why the same process could be the underpinning of infant mind, dreaming, and psychotic mind. Klein (1946) gave the pathological name paranoid-schizoid position to a mental process that bears much similarity to Freud's primary process and she used the term "manic" to describe some of its operations, leaving the reader to wonder if she is expressing phenomena that are normal, pathological, or somehow both.

Designation of psychopathology is a social judgment. Few if any of the designated psychiatric diagnoses have a demonstrable pathological physical correlate. The "medicalization" of psychiatry is based upon a diagnostic and statistical manual (DSM) constructed by a committee of psychiatrists based on periodic review and revision of what behavioral conditions are considered pathological. Homosexuality is perhaps the most egregious example. Moreover, designation of mental illness requires either self-referral for treatment or consensus labeling and related social action, medical or legal. However much some people may dislike what Trump does and says, a large proportion of the population seem to support him, at least at the time of this writing, and he certainly does not believe he has a mental problem. Even more striking is the fact that his mental activity and language have proven remarkably adaptive in a broad social context, so that far from finding himself in the consulting room of a psychiatrist because of personal distress or because he has been taken there after a destructive collision with a representative of social law, he can remark that he is the president, in charge of the most powerful nation on earth, and we are not, confidently proclaiming that whatever distress he feels is the product of the misbehavior of others. With regard to his language and rhetoric, his effect on crowds is remarkable and often during his presidential campaign had the earmarks of induced states of ecstasy and frenzy characteristic of a Dylan concert or a religious revival. He forcefully asserts things that are factually untrue so often that others come to believe that they are true and begin to act and think like undifferentiated clones. During his campaign he referred repeatedly to his opponent, Hillary Clinton as a criminal and the crowds came to chant "Lock her up," much like the rhythmic musical responsive chanting at a religious revival meeting. But just as we cannot label Dylan or the born again minister pathological, at this writing there is no basis to do so with President Trump.

It may ultimately prove to be the case that the language he uses is not adaptive to the demands of the presidency of the United States. If that should come about it would not be because he is functioning in primordial consciousness but because the political office he occupies requires reflective rational thought. It would also be because of the destructive, maladaptive content that is being expressed. In chapter 11 I speculate that such content is the consequence of earliest experiences during the attachment phase in which a distorted and destructive sense of self was formed. Whether his personality is ultimately labeled normal or abnormal depends on another matter, namely the judgment society makes of him. Just as an arm or a leg can be used for many purposes it is not possible to conclude from the presence of primordial consciousness alone whether the phenomenon in question is normal, aberrant, or pathological.

Language may be labeled aberrant under two conditions. The first is that there is miscommunication based on the inability of the speaker to recognize and take into account the inappropriateness of the language of primordial consciousness to the social and interpersonal context in which it is being employed. The second is that the meanings of the words and phrases that comprise the language of primordial consciousness express distorted beliefs about self and world resulting from pathology of the primary attachment process. Chapter 11 elaborates the role of pathology of early attachment in the development of a distorted sense of self and world: the particular content of the mother tongue of primordial consciousness that characterizes aberrant language.

It is paradoxical that at least in some instances, what may on the surface seem most bizarre may not be aberrant, and some instances that may on the surface seem entirely normal will, on deeper analysis, turn out to be aberrant. I have illustrated instances of the former. In chapter 13 I illustrate an instance where the apparent bizarreness does reflect language aberration, and in chapters subsequent to that, instances where the aberration only becomes apparent under the microscopic lens of a psychoanalytic encounter.

Chapter 11
Language aberration in relation to pathology of early attachment

Primordial consciousness and its language is a fundamental aspect of one's sense of self, like arms are a fundamental part of the body. When employed in inappropriate settings and ways that are destructive it is also a necessary component of language aberration. While arms are essential to give someone a hug or stab them with a knife, their mere presence does not determine in what way they are used. So it is with the relationship between primordial consciousness, language aberration, and psychopathology. Distortion of the sense of self and other as a consequence of pathology of attachment, the encoding of such distortion in the language of primordial consciousness, and the subsequent use of the language of primordial consciousness in an interpersonal/social setting where it is incongruent or discordant with implicit social expectations, are the essential components of language aberration. However, language aberration is not equivalent to a diagnosis of psychopathology. Determination of whether the resultant phenomenology is pathological is a matter of social judgment, and that, in turn, is the result of a person's quest for professional help (internal definition) or behavioral disharmony with social norms and expectations of such magnitude as to create a collision that produces a social judgment, for example breaking of the law (external definition).

Other than extreme instances such as the language of persons diagnosed schizophrenic, which I have dubbed "schizophrenese," language aberration may go unnoticed if parties to an interaction are under the illusion that they are dealing with a similar "reality" and communicating in reflective symbolic thought, and there are no obvious maladaptive consequences.

In order to set the context for development of aberrant language during the attachment phase and its relation to maternal pathology, it is necessary to review the maternal contribution that is required in order that the infant should form a secure attachment and accurate sense of self and world. Before doing so it is important to deal with the moralistic overload that has unfortunately been attached to the central importance, positive as well as negative, of the mother on all our development. Pathology in the initial relationship is not the same as social judgment of goodness or badness. And conversely, there is no doubt that development within normal limits can occur when the primary caregiver or caregivers are others than mother. However, the mother's impact for good or ill cannot be matched by others because some of the most profound effects of the first relationship that involves the development of primordial consciousness begin *in utero* during the final trimester of pregnancy and gestation, if not sooner. So for the purposes of discussion, based on evidence that the contribution of the biological mother is unique, I focus on her. At the same time I want to make clear the distinction between causal accountability and social judgment and blaming.

Mother must be attuned, responsive, and accurate with regard to perceiving her infant's uniqueness and differentiating his signals from those coming from her own separate self. She must be able to move flexibly between her own life as a separate person in reflective representational thought and the undifferentiated state of primordial conscious fusion with her infant. Then she can provide responsive holding and emotional security; the stable foundation for her infant to develop a sense of self as well as the basis from which the infant can develop the second language based on the recursive ability to reflect on oneself and the world and to accurately represent and differentiate body sensations, emotional experience, and external reality. Mothers whose own attachment phase was problematic may not be able to provide such a stable base.

The pathological attachment process that produces aberrant language most likely begins in the last trimester of intrauterine life, gaining power throughout the first year, especially the first six months, of life, and gradually attenuating by age 5 or so, at which time the impact of primordial consciousness on language would seem more or less complete.

In chapter 9 I mentioned the seminal contribution of John Bowlby, the founder of what has come to be known as attachment theory. Mary Ainsworth (1982; Ainsworth, Behar, Waters, & Wall, 1978), his best known student devised a way to study his propositions called the "strange situation" experiment. It led to classifying infant attachment behavior into four affect-driven categories, a motivational proposition consistent with the characteristics of primordial consciousness. These are: secure, anxious/avoidant, ambivalent/resistant and disorganized/disoriented. Mothers of ambivalent/resistant infants were themselves insensitive and unpredictable, but not rejecting. Their infants were anxious and passive at home, and in the strange situation preoccupied with mother and her whereabouts while also being anxious and confused. Mothers of anxious/avoidant infants were rejecting of their infants' attachment behavior and their infants were anxious and angry, intolerant of separations. In the strange situation they insisted on exploration and tended to ignore mother. The other category, disorganized/disoriented, was elaborated by Ainsworth's student and collaborator, Mary Main. Mothers of disorganized/disoriented infants were frightening, and their infants, caught in an approach-avoidance conflict, manifested disorganized and disruptive behavior that included their language. Main comments on one such peculiarity of language relevant to primordial consciousness, namely the presence of contradictions in their speech (Hesse & Main, 2000, p. 1117).

Lyons-Ruth (2003), and the Boston Change Process Study Group (BCPSG) (Stern et al., 1998) also formulated a model of disorganized attachment. They concluded that if caregivers behave in ways that are rejecting and attacking, and distort the meaning of infant initiatives by responding to them with dissonant or inappropriate affects, their infants will manifest in new learning situations with others the kind of maladaptive and self-destructive responses that might have been adaptive responses to their mothers' behavior. Perhaps this could be looked upon as an early manifestation of transference.

As one might imagine, most of the neuroscientific studies of language acquisition have focused on the positive and constructive things that good enough mothers do reflexively to engage first their fetuses and then their infants in the task of becoming sentient selves. There are a few studies of mothers with diagnosed pathology. A study of depressed mothers and their 3–4-month-old infants indicated less attunement and responsiveness and less flexible use of "motherese" (Bettes, 1988). Another study, of 6- and 10-month-old infants with depressed mothers, found that their mothers were less responsive, less affectively involved, and that their responses were not as attuned (Herrera, Reissland & Shepherd, 2004). A study comparing hospitalized schizophrenic mothers with mothers with postnatal hospitalizations for other reasons concluded the schizophrenic mothers used motherese less frequently (Wan, Penketh, Salmon & Abel, 2008). These results are hardly surprising. What are the consequences for the infants, and their development of primordial consciousness, reflective representational thought, and sense of self?

Anna-Maria Rizzuto uses clinical illustrations to focus on the relationship of language aberrations to what was learned in the attachment phase without the attendant assumption that Freud, Klein, von Domarus, Winnicott, and others made, which I commented on in chapter 10, that the form of the mental process is what is abnormal. Rizzuto writes, "When the pleasure in verbal communication has been substituted by disrupted exchanges, the wish to speak may be diminished or intensely defended against (2002, p. 1333). She states that "The specific difficulties encountered by different analysands in the effort to free associate result not only from their conflicted wishes and fantasies but also from a reawakening of problems encountered with parents and family in the course of speech acquisition" (p. 1339). She cites an interesting example, not unlike ones I present in subsequent chapters, in which her anorexic patient said: "I don't listen to what you say. Those are only words!" (p. 1334). In describing this patient she writes:

> When the child's emotional integration lags behind the developmental appearance of the pronoun *I* as a linguistic tool, a dissociation may take place between the conversational *I* and the psychical. That was the case with my bulimic patient quoted briefly above, who *experienced* herself as an *I* for the first time during analysis. She said: "It is the first time in my whole life that I have said *I* and meant it." (Rizzuto, 1988, p. 378)

The bodily consequences of her psychically owned – not just linguistic – *I* experience were immediate: she did not have to overeat and was able to look at her naked body in the mirror for the first time, feeling that "My body from the neck down truly belongs to me." (p. 379) "Up to that point, she had felt that she lived in her head, behind her eyes." (Rizzuto, 2003, pp. 300–301)

In the essay on her unusual language in chapter 15 Jane comments on a similar experience. Rizzuto's example illustrates the difficulty developing the language of separation and reflective representational consciousness but does not describe the mental process that her patient did use, and implies that language actually had no meaning for her, rather than that her language was qualitatively different.

Mothers who are not attuned and responsive to infant signals or who do not have their own issues sufficiently differentiated from those of their infants will misperceive and mistakenly respond (or fail to respond) in ways that combine distortion, hostility and rejection. Some mothers doubtless, and most likely unwittingly, sing negative affect tones to their fetuses and subsequently to their infants, much of it in privacy where no one else can hear. Such songs of anger and rejection may have to do with the meaning to the mother of being pregnant and with real, imagined, and anticipated problems. Fetal needs may be perceived as hostile attacks draining mother's body. Mothers who do not differentiate themselves accurately from others may attribute to the fetus malevolent threatening qualities and affects not owned in themselves. Recently a woman who I believe was basically a devoted mother reminisced about her very real concerns, based on miscarriages in prior pregnancies, that she was going to miscarry again, and the extraordinary lengths she went to in hopes this would not happen. She recalled talking to the fetus in the late stages of pregnancy although she was not certain in retrospect how much was actually spoken aloud and with what intonation, saying "You're on your own now, kiddo; I've done everything I can." An unwitting song of disengagement if not rejection.

Returning to President Trump, whose language of primordial consciousness and a solipsistic universe was described in chapter 10, what distinguishes his language as aberrant resides in its perseverative use in situations where the mature language of awareness of a world of separate others, is to be contextually assumed of a person in that office. I emphasize that in what follows I am not equating his aberrant use of language with psychopathology and I am not making a diagnosis. That would require a consensus social judgment which would doubtless disqualify him from office, and as I write this book that crucial element is missing.

However well he covers it with formal language of caring which, however, seems to reflect no emotional substance as it is disjunctive with his actions that seem to be based mostly on unrepresented hatred and lack of respect for the separateness of others, I wonder where President Trump acquired the dystopian view of himself as beleaguered in a world in which he is surrounded by enemies, plots and deception. Why does he assume that any truly separate person, who does not totally echo or mirror his views, radically inconsistent and changeable though that person may be, is his enemy? What is the significance of his relentless urge to remind others how great he is, how he knows best, and how he is always right? Where did he develop the need to acquire vast riches and control enormous military power as well as his apparent phobia of contamination in order to isolate and defend himself against attack? While we have no direct evidence about how he assimilated such a view, the fact that it is expressed in the language of primordial consciousness, which involves actualization of a worldview, rather than as something to be reflectively thought about, suggests that it may have arisen during the attachment phase in which the potential for separateness from mother was experienced as dangerous. This may have left him without the secure validated sense of self necessary to move to the predominant use of reflective representational thought and to a world where self and others are perceived as separate differentiated entities.

In fact Trump's peculiar use of personal pronouns bears remarkable similarity to phenomena observed in the pronouns of normal infants in the first years of life who are negotiating the transition between the state of psychological undifferentiation and the acquisition of a separate sense of self and others as described in chapter 9. Consider, again, his gaffe at the award ceremony for Native American code talkers that I described in chapter 7. He stated: "We have a representative in Congress who they say was here a long time ago. They call her Pocahontas. But you know what, I like you." As it was Trump who used "Pocahontas" as an epithet for Elizabeth Warren we would expect to hear a subjective "I" of acknowledgement but instead he speaks as an undifferentiated "we" and "they." His concluding "I" contradicts his use of the epithet demeaning Native Americans only seconds before. Trump uses "I" appropriately when referring concretely and operationally to things he did or intends to do but has difficulty when it involves acknowledging his own problematic behavior. On other occasions when one would expect that he refer to himself as "me" or "I" he speaks as though he were another person, referring to Donald Trump. On May 4, 2009, he wrote: "Be sure to tune in and watch Donald Trump on Late Night with David Letterman as he presents the Top Ten List tonight!" And on May 9, 2017, he tweeted that the ". . . Trump/Russia story was an excuse used by the Democrats as justification for losing the election. Perhaps Trump just ran a great campaign?" He regularly refers to the author of presidential actions he has taken or intends to take by fiat as "we."

Little detail is known about those early years of Trump's infancy and most of that from a three generational history of the Trump family (Blair, 2000). While he talks of his stormy relationship with his autocratic father and the incorrigible behavior that led his father to send him to military boarding school at age 13, he has never had much to say about his mother, and neither he nor she has ever conveyed to others the sense that they were close. His mother must have gotten pregnant with his younger brother in the middle of Donald's second year of life. His mother had postpartum hemorrhaging necessitating an emergency hysterectomy after the birth of his brother when Donald was about 2½ years of age, subsequent to which she had four more surgeries in close proximity for septicemia, and presumably a prolonged and physically difficult recovery. His older siblings were informed by their father that mother might die, but there is no information from the book that Donald's emotional needs were taken into account. It is notable that this trauma came at the age at which pronoun use is developing; the developmental juncture between the psychological – not functional cognitive – state of undifferentiation from others and the condition of separation and individuation in which pronouns reflect the distinction between "I" and "thou."

As an adult Trump has had numerous relationships with women, marital and extramarital, and many women have accused him of making unwanted sexual advances to them. In light of the history of maternal disruption and deprivation and an attendant sense of powerlessness that can be inferred from this minimal information, the contents of a 2005 recording he made that was released during the course of his presidential campaign, are of interest. In it he said that a celebrity like him "can do anything" to women, including "just start kissing them . . . I don't even wait" and "grab 'em by the pussy."

Contrast Donald Trump's view of the world with that of Bob Dylan, whose creative use of primordial consciousness was discussed in chapter 7. The themes of many of Dylan's songs also express terrible things happening in a world where many are oppressed, but they come from a perspective of people caring about one another and coming together, in a socio-centric "family" of brother- and sisterhood.

Primordial consciousness may persist in older children and in situations where it is not contextually appropriate because the mind and sense of self have been so severely traumatized by distortions and failures during the attachment phase that the person lacks a sufficiently secure sense of self to separate from mother and not be terrified by her and by the world of differentiated others that in the infant's undifferentiated mind she represents. One of the major characteristics of primordial consciousness is that it is the language of an undifferentiated non-separate self. This quality may have been more adaptive to a situation of helpless infant dependence on a hostile, rejecting, invalidating or indifferent mother; a situation in which awareness of being a separate person would have been intolerably threatening.

Returning to President Donald Trump, one of the most striking features of the vignettes I presented is his utter undifferentiated even grandiose conviction there is no other point of view than his own, and that he is always right. A hypothesis worth entertaining is that remaining in this undifferentiated state is protection against the threat of being in a world of separate other people who are misperceived as being intolerably dangerous.

One of the characteristic features of primordial consciousness in language aberration is to form words that on the surface seem ordinary but on close scrutiny are undifferentiated from the idiosyncratic content learned during the attachment phase. For example, Dr. Rizzuto's patient used language with presumptively shared meaning, but nonetheless at a deep level believed words lacked the meaning they have to others. An example of a situation where commonly accepted meanings in reflective representational thought differ from the idiosyncratic meanings of someone speaking in primordial consciousness comes from the manner in which pronouns are used in affectively loaded interpersonal situations. While the second and third person pronouns may seem to imply sharing with a separate person they may actually be expressing the undifferentiated state: content the subject is not fully aware is in his or her mind, so that in reality they are "I" or "me" conceptions disguised as sharing. And the absence of that capacity to reflect is often indicated by the use of the first person pronoun "I" to express agency or being rather than self-awareness.

The meaning of basic relational concepts including such things as caring, love, anger, separation and the like may have been defined in a socially inverted way during the attachment phase as well, so that protestations of love, for instance, are applied to situations that might more consensually and objectively be described as hateful or rejecting. Vivid examples of this can be found in Lisabeth's essay in chapter 16 and Jacob's in chapter 17. Finally, the words used to describe images do not refer to stable continuous emotionally based mental representations, for instance fantasies or memories, but are more like evanescent snapshots whose emotional and historical significance has not been processed. Jacob, in chapter 17, describes this process clearly.

Remembering events from this early period in the course of analysis is difficult or impossible because the mother language of primordial consciousness in which they have been encoded lacks the capacity for reflection, representation, and logical integration, hence does not support memory, and because the meaning of the content available to the person is so often misleading. Reconstruction, however, is possible through the laborious process of mature translation of diffuse affects, body sensations, gestures, facial expressions, enactments and the like, as they arise in the transference of the psychoanalytic encounter. The essays that comprise chapters 13–17 demonstrate that in instances where no caring bond is formed during the initial attachment phase, the infant is unable to form a separate self-sense based on recognition and valuation of bodily experiences, perceptions and nascent emotions. Instead it assimilates a defensive undifferentiated identity (not to be confused with more mature selective identifications) with the destructive characteristics of the mothering person, insuring a kind of safety from the threat of separation through camouflage.

One significant problem in relating disturbances of infantile attachment to aberrations in adult language uses is the absence of longitudinal studies of the same individuals linking these two phases of life. Correlating similarities is not the same as demonstrating causal linkages. Perhaps in the future it will be possible to conduct longitudinal studies of mothers and infants beginning in the prenatal period and involving long-term follow-up.

Chapter 12
Clinical methodology and data

In the chapters to come I present data to illustrate my hypothesis about language development and aberration in the form of essays written by five current and former patients on the subject of what they learned about their aberrant language use during the course of psychoanalytic therapy.

Data that aspires to be scientific has been classified into two categories, nomothetic and idiographic. Clinical case data is idiographic, and many have questioned whether such data is indeed "scientific." These are concepts coined by the Kantian philosopher Wilhelm Windelband and introduced to American psychology by Gordon Allport (1937). Idiographic reasoning and idiographic data is consistent with general systems theory. It is nonlinear and nonquantitative, based on the idea that the mind of a human being is a complex dynamic system that cannot be analytically reduced to linear quantitative causal propositions and conclusions. From this perspective subjective descriptions, such as the ones this study is based upon, are "legitimate" data as are the conclusions reached from dynamic systemic analysis of them, even though they are neither linear nor quantitative.

But as with any research data, not all idiographic data is equally valid. What constitutes legitimate idiographic (clinical) data? Clinical material used to illustrate and validate theoretical propositions usually consists of vignettes selected and described by the author analyst intended to convince an audience of fellow analysts of the validity of a particular hypothesis; what I call secondary data. Although brief quotations, the accuracy and contextual relevancy of which must be taken on faith, may be included, this is not primary data and is fraught with problems of subjectivity, absence of sufficient content to ascertain internal consistency, and biases of selection and translation. Its most obvious limitation, however, is that it does not come directly from the patient in the form of an independent response to or elaboration of the problem about which the analyst is writing. And what is attributed to the patient can never be independently corroborated as accurate and sufficient. We must accept on faith the analyst's description of the patient and their interaction, and of particular relevance to a study of language and its aberrations the patient's language is not available except in those occasional selected quotes; we only read the language of the analyst into which it has been translated.

It is difficult to study language aberrations without direct access to patient language, difficult to present verbatim recorded accounts without violating privacy and confidentiality and adding an immeasurable distortion factor to their interaction, and difficult to know how to deal with the enormous amount of material in just a single hour, even if it is available. In 1996 I abstracted years of detailed notes I had made after individual sessions and produced five lengthy reports of cases, from start to finish. In 2003 I enlisted the help of Caroline, the woman with a schizophrenic diagnosis who had begun to be aware of her language peculiarities, and she allowed me to write down verbatim accounts of some of her utterances and then she tried to translate them into "ordinary English." Her original translations and her essay about her language written at a time, fifteen years later, when she had acquired further insight, comprises chapter 13. Over the years I have worked with a number of persons who have learned about their unusual uses of language as a result of growing reflective self-awareness. So I decided to base this study on direct accounts from a selected group of patients, presented in their own words. This method is not without problems of its own, of course. Are these really the patients' views or are they reflections of my own and illustrations of unanalyzed transference issues?

I chose six patients, some currently in treatment and others not, with whom I had worked in intensive psychoanalytic therapy for a number of years, in whose treatment discussions of language usage had played a prominent role. This very fact, of course, suggests a bias and focus of mine in the consulting room that another analyst might not have. In each of these persons psychotic mentation, defined as a preponderance in the transference (and in outside reported relationships) of the mentation of primordial consciousness expressing distorted views about self and other, dissociated from mature regulation and control by reflective representational thought, played a significant role. In some instances it was concealed by a false self, to use Winnicott's (1965) term, or as I would put it, with a facility for using reflective representational thought, albeit in circumstances where it was not linked with the patient's core emotional self but was being used for instrumental purposes as part of a psychotic personality organization. In some it played a more subsidiary role and in others, like Caroline, it took the form of blatantly obvious delusional and hallucinatory experiences. Each of these persons had come a long way in self-awareness of his or her primordial conscious mentation and resolution of the psychotic problems its use presented, and was able to reflect on it articulately. Some of these people were contacted post-termination while in other instances I looked for an opportune moment when we were discussing language to introduce the subject of my interest and ask if the person would agree to write an account of what he or she had learned. My request was greeted with varying degrees of enthusiasm, ambivalence, and even hostility, but in each instance stimulated productive analytic work. Of course I tried as best I could to indicate that "no" would be an acceptable response, and since my patients generally have little difficulty expressing anger and negation toward me I believe that my effort was at least somewhat successful.

Each of the patients I contacted initially agreed to write an essay and five of the six completed the task. The sixth, who had terminated treatment, was not able to do so. The five responders provided me with remarkable insightful essays, as you will see. What I found of note was that regardless of the extent of ambivalence about writing the essay each one expressed the retrospective conviction that it had been a very positive learning experience. In fact some decided in the months after completing the project that they had new ideas and went back to write more for their personal edification.

Patient essays

Chapter 13
Caroline
Schizophrenese

Caroline's florid psychosis emerged shortly after she had somehow managed to graduate from college in what I suspect was an instance of social promotion. She became catatonic after dining in a restaurant, requiring the first of numerous hospitalizations. Many years later she told me she had been waiting for Prince Charming to come and take care of her, as mother had promised during her prepubertal years during which the two of them spent much time in mother's bed watching television soap operas. She spent much of the first decade of her adulthood, subsequent to that episode and prior to my meeting her, in mental hospitals and halfway houses, in retrospect "perfecting" a sense of identity as disabled and successfully conveying to others the expectation that she was not competent to care for herself and they needed to take care of her. She was delusional and hallucinating, in various states of regression, one so severe that she was catatonic and had to be tube-fed, bathed, and carried to the bathroom. Of particular relevance to her language, at one time she clamped her teeth on her tongue, almost biting it off before her jaws could be pried apart. Many years later she was able to explain to me that it was because she did not want to speak to her parents; a literal enactment of the aphorism "I bit my tongue."

Two courses of electroconvulsive therapy were followed by numerous medications and psychotherapy with a psychoanalyst, but the more "treatment" she was given the worse she seemed to get. Her delusional sense of identity, which once again I only learned about many years subsequently, was based on the belief she was special friend, lover, or potential bride of the idealized doctors and other mental health personnel who took care of her. She interpreted their dedication to their work literally to mean that they loved destructive disabled patients, and the goal was to gain their attention and win their undying love and care by being crazier than any of her fellow patients. Naturally and unbeknown to them, the more attention staff gave her the worse she got, and eventually the hospital administrators concluded that they had nothing more to offer her and transferred her to McLean Hospital, accompanied by the written comment by her doctor that she was a "pathetic young woman." There I agreed to the request of the ward administrator to try to work with her. Caroline was diagnosed schizophrenic by the DSM III criteria which were current at that time.

When we were introduced, Caroline's attractive and childishly cheerful demeanor, which I learned was typical of her staff contacts, seemed markedly at odds with her destructive regressive history, leading me to smugly fantasize, as I am sure others had done before me, that I could rescue her whereas others had failed. Soon after her admission Caroline broke into the locked medication room on the ward and consumed a large quantity of drugs before being apprehended. She remained comatose and near death for several days. Subsequently she revealed to me her belief that the emergency room physician who may have saved her life was entranced by her nude body on the gurney and wanted to marry her, a belief that became the basis for a many years long delusional obsession with that doctor. Many years later she explained to me that she had been unable to tolerate the idea that she was like the other psychotic, dilapidated patients who inhabited the ward, so she decided to *get in* with the nurses and doctors. "So I *broke in* to the med. room. I was going to *get in*, maybe like the nurses, to their power." It reminded her of how she was unable to *get in* with her parents as a child because they were so *out of it*. She had felt similarly *outcast* at college. The terms *getting into* and being *out of* had become identical to bodily action on her environment that she endowed with the power to alter reality.

She remained hospitalized during our first two years of work, and her destructive behavior required long stays in a barren seclusion room. In these and many other ways I gradually learned that her worldview, likely acquired from two parents who used their wealth to insulate themselves from ordinary requirements of reality testing, self-control and responsibility, was one of entitlement; that she was exempt from the rules that governed others, that her destructive behavior was the ticket to getting taken care of, and that it was the task of others to do so. She navigated a course combining impulsive self-gratification with destructive regressive behavior, which I gradually came to realize was driven by the diffuse rage she was unaware of. A model of sweetness in superficial conversations, during one on one interactions with caregivers such as myself whom she professed to idealize, she attacked and blamed others for their failure to take care of her while attributing to them many of her own undesirable characteristics that in her undifferentiated state she was unable to acknowledge.

Twelve years of analytic therapy ensued, the first two of which were spent in the hospital, prior to the vignettes I next describe. Caroline's seductive ineptitude made hospital staff feel needed and special. Her days were spent describing in minute detail, to any staff member who would listen, everything she was doing, conveying the impression she knew nothing and could not make up her own mind about anything and that the helper of the moment was the special person who could rescue her by filling her empty head with his or her advice. In fact Caroline used these contacts as opportunities to evacuate rather than consolidate the contents of her mind, and she paid little attention to any of the extensive advice she was given, although she made it all into slogans that she took with her so that she seemed at times like an encyclopedia of banal bumper stickers. Her seemingly naïve show of interest and what superficially seemed like idealization, including flattering the current caregiver in comparison to the others who failed or harmed her, effectively concealed what I gradually came to realize was her enormous rage and arrogant contempt toward the helper of the moment. Despite how easy it was to be blinded and seduced into collusion by her flattery – I was the greatest therapist – I began to catch on to her maneuver and I gradually learned she was bad-mouthing me to other staff and that when I said something she did not wish to hear, she told other staff that I was literally hitting her. Bizarre as that may sound, many staff were convinced I was harming her and responsible people began to suggest that I was responsible for her regressive behaviour and that I be removed as her therapist.

At first I mistook Caroline's repetitious statements that nothing good would ever happen for expressions of despair and hopelessness. But as she repeatedly destroyed every opportunity to be constructive about her life, I began to realize that her words were not to be taken at face value as expressions of despair but reflected a sense of determination, and that concealed beneath her sweet, incompetent façade was enormous rage – a drive to despoil whatever was given her. Staff members believed that the more anxious, confused, scattered and upset Caroline appeared, the more of their caretaking she needed. The squeaking wheel got lots of grease, but paradoxically it moved slower and slower. The director of the hospital eventually suggested she might be transferred to a state hospital where life would be much more Spartan than at McLean, and perhaps this motivated her to be a bit more constructive. After a time she was able to move out of the hospital to a halfway house. Although she periodically longed for the good old days of irresponsibility in the hospital, she never returned. And although her inclination and capacity for independent living and for work remained marginal, it slowly improved. Along the way she created every kind of problem imaginable, and came near to suicide, serious accidents, trouble with the law, destitution and starvation. After years of treatment we uncovered her unconscious envy of homeless street-corner mendicants, for to her they represented success in presenting a disabled identity and getting others to take care of them, thereby absolving them of any responsibility.

Our sessions typically consisted of Caroline's pressured evacuation of all the events of her life since we had last met, along with descriptions of the problems she had got herself into. "Just one more thing" was a favorite response when I would attempt to get a word in of my own; and when she was not able to avoid my comments about her responsibility she was full of plans and pledges to do better, none of which ever came to fruition. She made intensive efforts to seduce me into participating in a mind-losing sexual orgy in which she could imagine our identities merged through my penis, so that by deluding herself she was me and I her she would get what she imagined I had. My efforts to contain and to help her to focus were, for the most part, either ignored or greeted with rage and blaming. When I resisted her blandishments, which required self-control as she was an attractive and at times seductive woman, she would become seriously abusive and hint to others, including her family, not only that I was an irresponsible and ineffective therapist but also that she was an innocent victim whom I was fooling into believing that I was a good therapist and that I was keeping her as my patient in order to satisfy my greed and get the family money.

As years went by Caroline took small steps toward personal autonomy. There were miniscule increments of insight, and even an occasional sense of productively working together; but these were regularly undone and destroyed. Increasingly I came to feel the treatment was stalemated. Shortly prior to the events I will describe she appeared to regress and behave like a typical chronic schizophrenic, with flattened affect, wooden facial expression, a gross tremor which I feared related to her current antipsychotic medication, and such paralytic ambivalence that at times she could hardly move, but sat rocking back and forth. I experienced overwhelming lethargy during our sessions. I tried to believe, and to tell Caroline, that she was offering me a lethal dose of the kind of overwhelming despair she had not been able to bear in the course of her futile childhood efforts to relate to absent regressed parents but my interpretations had no substantive effect on either of us.

Although there had always been noticeable peculiarities in her language, I had not focused attention on them other than to tell her on occasion that I did not understand and to ask her to clarify. One day, in a poorly concealed moment of exasperation and without much thought, I remarked that she was speaking schizophrenese, a language I did not comprehend. She was taken aback, and informed me that as I was the therapist and *she* was the schizophrenic, it was *my* job to understand her. This was prior to the coinage by cognitive linguistic neuroscientists of the language with which mothers address their infants as "motherese," both languages being manifestations of primordial consciousness.

After unproductive discussions that spanned several sessions I had the liberating thought that whether or not she chose to learn from me, I was not trapped in a hopeless situation. I could terminate with her or learn about language from her and maybe write a paper! I suggested she could teach me about schizophrenese, implying, of course, that she did not have to give it up. In situations where hitherto I would have felt hopeless, angry and bored, I pulled out pad and pen, and in a state of rapt attention to what she was saying, acted like a student asking the professor to explain the lecture, an attitude that left her a combination of surprised, fascinated and amused, I took the verbatim notes that, years later, she gave her permission for me to use as data for my 2003 paper *Language and Delusion in Schizophrenia.* To my surprise, my self-serving action finally got Caroline's attention when what I thought had been my efforts to care about her had not succeeded, and she began to show some interest in and capacity to reflect about her own mind. Caroline began to alert me to get out my notebook when she sensed an urge to speak schizophrenese, and she decided to keep a journal of her utterances. When I once asked her, in response to her having just alerted me to get pen and notebook, how she was able to determine that she was about to speak schizophrenese, she replied, "It's when I put things together in strange ways that no one else would understand," adding, "I take a giant leap."

Here are some examples of the work that ensued. A question mark in parenthesis means I asked her to elaborate further about what she meant.

Caroline had gone to play pool after taking her car to be repaired. It had been damaged due to her irresponsible driving.

> I had time to kill. Rack it up and pocket 'em. Sock it and rock 'em. Clear the table. The only table that had monkey business to it. [?] E. [a staff member in the hospital] and I used to play pool. [?] Judgement Day. I've got so many balls and I have to put them in the pocket. Get the eight-ball in and you're out. I've got to shoot straight from the hip, and keep both feet on the ground. Just straight shots coming from the heart. People have things racked up against you but you keep on shooting, and if you make a racket like me it gives them more ammunition. [?] Now you *really* think I'm crazy. I racked 'em up and then I bought a root beer. The guy said, 'You can't drink that here,' and then we talked about getting 50% off lodging in [a distant resort]. I said that late September is the best time to go there. She laughs. [*What are you laughing about?*] Well, it's not a short walk to get there, and I have $16 in my wallet. They don't want unethical behavior in the bar. So I think about going there; I build up in my mind places to go. I start out thinking I'm going to clean the apartment. Then I do these other things. Then I start thinking when I don't that it's the fault of the landlord and others. Then I ran out of time and I had to go to work; I was late again. [*What about the resort?*] It's a *Closetland* place [a reference to a movie about a woman who turned to fantasy in order to endure torture]; no problems there, everything is fine.

A rendition in reflective representational thought might be:

> The Day of Judgment has come for me. I'm in a rage at myself for all my monkey business – damaging my car, not being financially responsible, not cleaning my apartment or being on time for my appointments, and treating life like a game. I give others ammunition to use against me. I've really got myself behind the eight-ball and I've got to get my feet back on the ground. But I'm in a rage at having to be responsible; I just want to kill more time, blame others, wipe the table clean of all my problems and imagine I'm at a resort on a perpetual vacation.

Instead of such a thoughtful reflective statement she describes an animated, literal – not metaphorical – pool table microcosm of which she is omnipotent master, as she combines words, body actions, and things. It is Judgment Day, and she literally believes she is ridding herself of her problems. Killing time involves rage-filled destructive action. It also reflects the absence of comparative concepts that would serve to make her aware of the passage of time and its implications, such as process, work, patience and perspective. What might appear to be low-grade metaphors or similes – clichés such as "shoot straight," "shoot from the hip," "rack 'em up," "rock 'em and sock 'em," being "behind the eight-ball," "killing time" – are actually action condensations of words, body movements and things.

Caroline regularly sent bizarre letters to a long list of people she had interactions with, past and present. She titled the letter that follows "The Class Act." She sent it to twenty-five of her former mental health caretakers as accompaniment to a Valentine card. It begins with the salutation "To a Quarter of Caring People."

> Although I have loving feelings for the people who have held me in their thoughts of care this card is an expression of appreciation and care not love. I am on an excavation of *dignity* (*dig–knit–tea*). The month of financial February is for my initial dig. The month of March, my birthday always and forever holding, is for my *knit*. The month of April is for a poem once learned as in college . . .
>
> > T. T. T.
> > See these three.
> > Hear their chime.
> > Things take time for thought, taxes and *tea*.

Her letter concludes with a paragraph of plans for each of the months of May and June. In response to my request that she explain this to me in ordinary language, she says:

> It's how overwhelmed I am about the coming months. In the sixth grade a teacher I respected took her class on an archeological dig. That means, 'dig in.' 'Dignity' has three parts: *dig–knit–tea*. You have to dig in and knit things and then drinking tea calms you down. [*But why do you say it this way, and not something like: 'I'm overwhelmed about how I'm going to manage my life in a dignified way during the coming months. I need to find a way to calm down and to use my sixth grade teacher as a model for digging in, working hard and pulling my life together'?*] The way *I* said it is brilliant. Besides, it keeps me at a distance from people; puts me in a separate space where they won't know what I'm talking about. I don't want people to know how much distress I'm in. [*So you're writing a letter of information about yourself, with all sorts of details about your life, to people you supposedly care about – but you want to conceal the real information from them?*] The time is so overwhelming I had to compartmentalize it into months so I could manage my mess. Then I send it to responsible people and they will take care of it; I'm filling up their mailbox, adding to their concern. So I gave it to my landlord to read, and he said, 'Take care.' I got furious. He was supposed to take care of it. I'm getting a misery out of it, getting to sit in some low-down place and not move out of it. Some people try to intimidate people; I *intimate* people. [*?*] Relationships are too difficult, so I word my way into

a relationship with letters. I'd like to work my way into your hearts without working my way in, and without mentioning things that would work my way out of your hearts.

Caroline is gradually able to re-present the thought behind her letter into an ordinary language statement, but even at the conclusion of the discussion she is still partly speaking schizophrenese. If she were able to speak ordinary language, she might say something like:
I would like to fool myself and the others in my life that this is really a Valentine about loving and feeling close to them, and a resolution not to be such a low-down person and to identify myself with constructive responsible people and to work hard to dig myself out from the mess I've made. But really this card expresses my wish to avoid the pain of my situation, to disown my problems and to force them inside others to take care of.

What sets the schizophrenese apart from the ordinary language version is that she is not expressing wishes, nor is she speaking metaphorically when she writes phrases like "digging in," being "low down," "keep me in your heart," "I give you my heart," or "knitting together the strands" of her life. Instead of working, which involves effort, patience, thoughtful reflection and bearing of distress, she engages in wording, an action discharge with magical significance that is its antithesis. An ordinary person might work at solving her problems while singing such song lyrics as "Pack up your troubles in your old kit bag," or "Pack up your troubles and send them all to me." When Caroline says "I send it ('my mess') to responsible people . . . I'm filling up their mailbox . . . I word my way into a relationship with letters," she literally believes she is digging out and packaging her word-self into the Valentine card and putting it in the mailbox-hearts of people who in her undifferentiated world will hold and care for her emotionally distressed self in a way that she refuses to try to do. There is nothing left for her to think about, to feel, or to work on. In so far as her actions succeed in burdening others with her worries and problems, her wishful belief in a sense comes true. Fooling others, so that they work to help her while she pretends to listen but does not, is a necessary part of fooling herself. The words "dignity" and "intimate" are neologisms; homophonic compounds that combine word, action and thing. Caroline hears what her landlord says in schizophrenese, as well, rejecting and forcing back inside her own self to take care of. Her construction of it as a rejection throws her into a rage, which she, in turn, conceals.

Caroline talks about a visit with her mother:

I walked around the lake with my mother when my affair with my college professor was going on. [In her early twenties she allowed him to photograph her nude with her legs spread apart, and to use her sexually in other ways, as part of gratifying his fantasy that he was doing these things to his daughter. The physical position enacted her belief that he was entering her and taking over her care; at the same time it enacted her unrepresented rage and contempt for him, much like sticking out one's tongue.] And I told her about it. So the last few days I found three lakes and walked around them. Three guys were on one dock. Things reminded me of the professor. Birds on an island in the first lake remind me of a man who didn't disclose that he was probably having other relationships – probably screwing other women, all those birds – but it was hard to keep my mind together walking around the big lake because it was so big; too big a place to keep my mind. Then these guys started flirting, playing with my mind. All three of those lakes make a penis; the end, the middle, the part you play with. [*Why did you do this?*] I did it so I could focus on a destructive relationship; I was trying to feel the feeling. But the lakes are such a big temptation to fall in it again. Walking around the smaller lake I could get more in touch with the feeling of loss and hurt, some of the feeling; but it wasn't satisfying. The bigger lakes were overwhelming and I didn't know why I was there anymore; I was trying to get into trouble. The birds on the big lake felt threatening; all the people he screwed; the things I didn't see. I was foolish; I start to realize it but then instead it becomes my mother fooled me, not what I did. My mother goes to [her winter vacation home] and spends time watching the birds. I feel betrayed. I went to the dock and saw two birds in a caged area; I felt caged. I wondered if those women were prostitutes and ended in jail. [?] I'm trying to deal with what happened in my twenties with the professor. Around the lake my mother and I walked and I told her. [Her mother blamed the professor and told Caroline not to worry about what she had done.] The lie was talking to my mother about it and my mother's lies. My interest in the lake is a recreation of the crime when something equals nothing and nothing equals something. The lively pond is a metaphor for my mind, and my difficulty containing limits and boundaries; staying in bounds and not destroying everything; attending to a straight line of thought. The kids represent how easily I'm distracted and take my mind off. The lake is a reference to my mind, and the tree is my interest in life. The tree and the birds are a blaming thing. People don't tell others about their affairs but they communicate inside themselves about it. My mind is the pond, the tree. Claustrophobia is how "in the dark" a part of me is. My thoughts versus my actions. I say one thing, make my pledges, then I go do another. Destructive. I'm terrified of the temptation to blow everything to bits. My tree is empty and alone; others have things in their branches. I can't walk a straight line; I veer off, so I try another planet. It's painful. I know if I can't stay on line in this little pond then I'll never get anywhere in the bigger issues in life; I can look at trees that seem more interesting but I have to be able to deal with what's here. [*Now you are speaking in metaphor; why don't you always?*] Metaphors take more responsibility, they are more connecting.

Caroline begins speaking about her trip in language that is undifferentiated, enactive rather than reflective, concrete, imagistic and idiosyncratic. Instead of using what she sees metaphorically to internalize emotional meaning she gets lost in the words and images in an undifferentiated way. But by the conclusion of our discussion the physical elements of her surroundings have become incorporated in metaphors. A more elaborate reflective representational thought translation, that supplements her efforts with other information in my possession but preserves her own words and phrases, might be something like this:

> I've been thinking about my affair with the professor; trying to return, so to speak, to the scene of the crime and find a different way, in my mind, to handle what I couldn't deal with then; but I keep falling into the same old patterns of thinking. I fell into sexual temptation and I lost my mind. I was "out of my tree." Did he fool me or did I fool myself? Afterward my mother and I took a walk; I was struggling whether to face my feelings of hurt, responsibility and guilt, or stay in the dark about what I had done, and deny that I was a fool. But I couldn't contain myself, I can't seem to "go straight." I fell into it again and spilled everything out to my mother. I deserved to be punished, but instead of making me feel like a jailbird or a prostitute she blamed him, and she made like it was nothing; now I'd like to blame her for that and not myself.

In such a thoughtful reflective language version there emerges an emotional, reflective self, replete with the symbolism and metaphor that is missing in a language that fuses words, things and actions. She fails to integrate and differentiate her mind from the geography around her. She walks around a lake and what she sees is not assimilated into her mind in the form of reflective thought as a symbolic or metaphorical representation of her mind, the loss of her mind, and the wishful temptation posed by the three men and her fantasies about playing with their genitalia. Instead, in primordial consciousness, the perceptions remain external as concrete images and the words for them. Similarly she cannot differentiate her thoughts from her perceptions of the tree and the cage. She fails to integrate her perceptions into thoughtful metaphors such as that she "flew the coop" rather than taking her punishment for behaving like a prostitute and being a jailbird. Instead the perceptions and words for them remain concrete fragmentary things. Of the three vignettes this reflects the most mental maturity in so far as Caroline is trying to think and bear emotions at the very same time as she experiences the omnipotent capacity to eliminate what needs to be thought about, represented and felt. Both efforts fail.

Fast forward fifteen or so years to the time of the current study. With some limited help from family, mostly around payment for therapy, Caroline was leading a more or less independent life and although her basic attitudes about herself and the world remained operative she had acquired some ability to reflect on them, recognize them as ideas rather than concrete mindless actions, consider their basically maladaptive nature, and to work on the discrepancy between them and what might be a more mature and satisfying way to live. She not only spoke schizophrenese much less, she had acquired the capacity to be curious and to think about her unusual uses of language. In the essay that follows that she titled "Steady reflections on my private thoughts and language"

Caroline's language essay

I made an association of my language, thought and feelings to M and M's so that I'd simply remember it, and a nice lady, from long ago during my treatment, gave out the candy M&Ms to people. The M and M stands for the book *Of Mice and Men* by John Steinbeck. A main character is Lenny who is obviously mentally challenged by retardation, not too bright, or has some disability – usually I'd ignore or avoid this character and pretend he's separate, out there and has no connections in common with me – even though his mental limitations are right in the open especially when he speaks, talks. He has a stunted language ability and skills. I was struck by this story mainly by the excellent acting of John M. who played Lenny. His protector George describes about Lenny that "If he sees something pretty, he wants to touch it." Then though he means no harm or hurt to a living being, when they react to his ignorant invasion, caress, petting, and move or struggle – it's too much information, stimulation and sensory output and Lenny ends up at best merely scaring them or at worst controlling them, keeping them from screaming – breaks their neck, kills them and doesn't have a clue what happened. I relate to the part of Lenny's disturbing difficulty with language and emotions. I associate with the part having to do with Lenny seeing something pretty and just wanting to touch it, not knowing his own strength, the sensations, the scattered feelings of confusion and control.

I make associations from what I hear or perceive around me that are not based in reality or have a real connection. They seem similar to plagiarizing except that plagiarism involves copying another's text, work and ideas usually to advance in the absence of one's own lack of knowledge and comprehension. With myself and my language, I don't want to advance, develop and grow even on the temporary stepping-stone of someone else's insight, effort and work. I utilize my language to distance myself away from others, to be disconnected or increasingly camouflaged. I change the colors of my personality, whereas now I hide behind my manufactured language curtain. I think that it is important for me to elaborate on my association process and behavior. I'm not normal in this way. I take words, thoughts and sentences and basically do what I want with them as far as meaning, distorting what I am reminded of. Usually I make my connections based on convenience, my own irresponsibility and having the world outside align itself with my perception. One example of this happened recently when I've been very tense and have been living more on the edge. With this situation as my stage I tend to justify, be angry and give myself an extended license to make associations and connections that are comrades to the theory of an easier, thoughtless way for myself and are convenient. If I told a young person that I swim and he responded that I (interesting; I mean "he") preferred exercising outdoors with active sports and he said it twice my verbal language association would be that he directed me to not swim. Other language associations of this kind often involve the word "should" until I am mentally catatonic. I hear someone else's words and I association the living daylights out of them until no more than a smolder of the embers remains.

Another way I use my maladaptive language is silence for an excruciating amount of time comparable to holding my breath underwater, at which time it follows that I gasped for air or in reality I excrete my pent up voice out to often unsuspecting beings. With this technique I am angry and in a rage in many ways. While I am silent, I consider myself to be excluded from others and an observer apart. My transition from quiet on the outside and increasingly noisy and upset on the inside to a calculated discharge of rage, rampant irrational feelings is a clear indication of my own internal, fiery volcano and the level known as responsibility with my aversion and discernment of both.

Another language style I exercise secretly on paper. That is, secretly for many people, however not invisible from the 15 to 30 people I periodically write. What I've done more than anything else is broadcast and advertise myself as a woman who has no shame, order and self-respect. It hasn't been as much the content of my excretions as the damage has been demeaning myself.

Another destructive use of language is speaking softly. I actually am carrying on a sort of conversation with another person, however, I don't make the effort to talk in any way that I can connect verbally with the other person. I do this because I don't want to be responsible for my words. I don't want to make an honest commitment to the person I am speaking to. In this way, I believe that I do have to be engaged. There are frequent times when I maintain silence for abnormal periods of time. I used to be able to hold my breath for extended moments on land and underwater. In my childhood I'd cope by being silent and at any age I do not like responsibility. To talk is to engage and take a position especially in a lawless, unfair environment, especially when I was most often criticized, corrected or wrong. I don't mean instructed to learn what the right thing or way was to do, I mean I lived amid a harsh dark insanity, my parents' and then my own.

The truth is that despite my valiant efforts to be in limbo, live in a no man's land, undetected and with characteristic whereabouts unknown, I'd say truthfully I am one of the most entitled people I know. My language snags some.

I had two destructive parents. In the beginning my mother did not nurse me in any way. Although she was older it was no excuse for the distance she created and maintained. My mother took the hospital drugs that anesthetized her female body parts during my actual birth. She did not breast-feed me and in fact hired a nursing nurse to breast-feed me for most of my most formative beginning years. She was not busy due to working on having a career. She was busy with her irresponsible outlets of casual games and hobbies. So my mother succeeded in removing the major sensory organ and connection between mother and baby. She obstructed and destroyed my access routes to growth, development and love.

I could systemically describe my father in one common word: absence, though he lived in the same house. There are psychological diagnoses which apply to my father accurately, and common addiction labels [he was an alcoholic]; however, because many people gravitate to them to get their head, brain or mind wrapped around the problem, I'd like to merely conclude that I found it virtually impossible to constructively do so. I tried in certain ways during both my child and adult years only to become destructive myself and joined in with his rage. My father was the nonstandard walking bomb or pack of dynamite ready to explode like the torpedo fireworks he'd hurl out of his second-story window at my childhood friends and I. My father was walking unpredictability, drama and terror for a newborn baby who has no security with her mother. Touching my father was a dangerous proposition which made for confusion. My normal cry was muffled and snuffed out. What remained of my whimpering voice, my sniffling sigh and the embers of my rage no one knew. It happened on the inside. So the beginning of my disturbed language has at its source my child origin of conspiracy, a secret hiding place. I couldn't compete against my father's hostility and voyeurism. I mistakenly believe that living in my silence would save me. It only removed me further from the warm real world and boiled my own anger to its height.

I spoke almost inaudibly around my parents because I did not want them to hear me. I did not want my thoughts and feelings through vocal words to hit into their external, uncaring and often hostile atmosphere. Also by speaking silently I did not have to touch and be stimulated by their vacant personal nonexistence. They decided not to exist so no different voice made me not exist too. When I talk I speak softly so that no one can hear me because that's my goal. To speak directly and so that the other person can actually hear and understand me requires me to be responsible for my words and actions, accountable and in a commitment. With my destructive parents, they were not accountable, responsible and honored no commitment to their only daughter. They never meant a word they said and they even spoke in a childlike gibberish that caused me to feel ashamed to be their girl and thus, ashamed of myself as well.

In my family with my destructive parents correspondence was crazy, for lack of a more formal word. My mother's notes were meaningless avenues to escape her awful situation and marriage. She wrote lists, jotted down reminder words usually in pencil and wrote my codependent letters while I was at a distant summer camp really meant as a device to keep me "in bed with her" which she did physically for a decade. My father blasted people with letters whereas I maintained a list of people I wrote what I referred to as Trail News for years. I thought my correspondence made sense and was a real way of connecting and touching caring professionals, family and a few friends. It was yet another empty vacancy in my broken life.

Since reality and connection are not strengths of mine, I associate with what I hear or perceive around me instead. In my childhood with my destructive parents, like many children who feel abandoned, I made up an imaginary world. The difference between myself and normal creative children was that since living in reality was unpopular in my family and I was painfully learning that there was nothing to connect to in order to survive, I imagined my pretend world and then lived in it. I manufactured my own secret language. I took up residence in my new habitat and vowed to exist and reside there until the bitter end. No one was going to discover me and my whereabouts.

I had difficulty learning to read in the second grade. This was after the books about Spot, Dick & Jane and the overhead written English alphabet in script and print. In second grade, I did not want to admit or let my teacher know I was having trouble reading. I didn't understand why the other students were reading fast and getting it and why my reading word by word or phonetically by individual consonant was wrong. Mrs. R who taught 6th grade caught me not doing my reading of *A Christmas Carol* and she noticed that when I tried to do my homework to present a little project on Amsterdam, especially Denmark, and Greek Civilization with Mesopotamia and King Ramesses I had substantial difficulty separating the actual texts, i.e. the factual contexts such as the encyclopedia's words from my own. It was as though I did not have any part of myself and mind which contained original thought or my own self. And I felt so angry and put upon by her instructions and insights that I cheated with my presentations. I copied word-for-word from the texts and onto my blank, index cards, and recited verbatim to deliver my presentation.

With more advanced education I often did not understand the subjects and discussion topics. Instead of acknowledging in talking to someone for better understanding, I'd seclude myself and isolate myself in places like library cubicles and try to cram and force words, language and knowledge into my brain. It did not work out well. Although I somehow barely graduated, I had a severe breakdown simultaneously.

I did not really understand what my psychotherapist in the Midwest was saying to me when he asked me to describe the voice I said I heard. I replied that I heard the word "jump." He took that to mean that I was determined to jump off a building. Because I was so utterly deflated and empty with my ability to think, have a language and express my thoughts and clear words, I went along and left him as the victor in that understanding [she attempted to jump out a hospital window]. In retrospect, I think my word from within, jump, meant that I was having a surge of energy and needed to jump ahead and keep moving on. These kinds of agreed resignations hurt me very much over many years. I was understood to be pathetic and I did not contest the falsity and allowed it to be an angry silence.

I was untouchable in my infancy and as a child. When I began working in therapy with Dr. Robbins as an inpatient he talked to me. I rejected his words and exclaimed to the caretakers and medical staff that he was hitting me because his words, caring therapeutic words felt and touched me as something new in my parched, untouched mind.

My thoughts and feelings were bound to erupt at some time. I committed my actual self destructive act shortly after being hospitalized. For a very long time,

I had secretly been constructing and digging an ineffective system of language and words within myself. It was as if I had a tunnel or trough inside me that was hollow, empty and echoed external stimuli. The tunnel and trough was the place within that was bare, naked and raw. It was the place where my language and words were supposed to have been formed, however with my being there was nothing and I could hide there. So, when I met Dr. Robbins he simply did his professional job and kept talking to me. The problem was that it hurt inside of me to have anyone talk to me and talk to the place that I have blocked off. It hurt that I did not have words and it hurt that I did not have my language and way of communication. Thus, having convinced the majority of the medical staff that I was a helpless, disability and in dire need of others and of little use by myself, I complained about Dr. Robbins, claiming he was hitting me and was too hard on me. He had merely asked for and tried to engage in communication with me. Since that time I still send my siren call to certain people to help helpless me and disrespect my therapist. The difference is that now I am aware of what I do and change my attitude and behavior. It's very sad when one of my characteristics is to criticize and get the gang together against the person who cares. I'm not proud of myself now like I once was.

By working with Dr. Robbins, and having this privilege, I can see how his work to help me construct my thoughts and feelings has provided a core from where my troughs of empty words and tunnel of a void in coherent language can build and connect. For a little over 25 years as an outpatient mental patient what I have thought has mattered more, what I have felt has gradually stuck with me and the language and words are finally formed from an inner construct versus a repetition or echo of whatever is happening externally has been a rough journey.

My words and language are not well today. I still speak softly because I don't want people to hear me and commit me to the words I say. I am not a responsible woman, i.e. fade, avoid and say a mixed up phrase of incoherency. However with the help of my therapist I have an internal base whereby I know who I am and in everyday conversations I talk pretty well.

I am writing about what has changed with my language. This piece is about my awareness. Before, in many years gone by, I really didn't notice or think about my language, voice and the difficulties I have expressing myself. I wrote a huge amount of correspondence that was a dumping of my spontaneous moods and feelings. It was all disconnected although I imagined that my "writing" was connecting me with other people when it was both distancing me and portraying me with more visible mental disturbance and no privacy. I became more and more aware because of some of my older, patient relations passing away literally and figuratively my unusual language revealed my character defects and attitude clearer to the few remaining acquaintances. Also, I discovered that people who said they cared for the most part did not and thought I had problems. By looking at the core truth of myself and my language holding and maintaining relationships, I painfully discovered my barren existence. I utilize my language and behavior as such to drive people away by confusion, incoherent utterances via my irate anger, and suppressed rage. Before, I didn't stop to notice; primarily, I suppose because I was too much a part of my own delusion and denial process and my investment in not wanting to take responsibility for myself and my own life. I've been able to "black-out" reality far more than most people. This used to be something I was proud of and considered to be an achievement; whereas, now it's a source of pain. I whittled or whacked my life to virtually nothing.

With my awareness now, though, I have not succeeded in turning my life around. By being able to think about what I've done with my angry, awkward and antagonizing language, I no longer express myself in as much of my destructive ways. However, at present I am aware of how unassertive I am, how much I do not verbally protect my own privacy and self, and how I live as a morphed middle-aged woman without practiced avenues of communication and any wellness with healthy connections. As a child and into my twenties, my relationship with my destructive father was a blueprint of mental and verbal abuse. I existed mentally suffocated and verbally battered and beaten to a pulp. Now, with the consistent help of my therapist, Dr. Robbins, I have taken years to arrive at a place whereby I've cut back exercising my own arsenal and dumping my rage in my blasts and blurbs on people. Unfortunately, I think at present I'm trying to live with the shame, pain and frustration of bearing my mindless language expression and feeling completely overwhelmed and inadequate to assert myself in connecting, healthy and caring ways many years after the destruction's been done, my few special passed relations, who I had a historical, understanding relationship with, who knew me in a real way, and assert myself with my own voice in a barrage or what I experience daily as a moment-by-moment avalanche of the unknown. Still, with my language, I choose not to assert myself because I do not want to take a stand and be known, and responsible for what position I may voice. It has been a better way to cope for me than to be obstructed, criticized and "wrong," inferior. Nonetheless, as Mrs. Eleanor Roosevelt said, "No one can make you feel inferior without your permission." My destructive father gave me his lawless license to join in with his own irresponsible ways. My paternal bully never once told or encouraged me to know that I had my own sense of permission and a mind of my own.

Discussion

Caroline uses an ordinary vocabulary and sentence structure although some of the sentences she makes seem so strange as to mask this fact. The meaning of the language is idiosyncratic. Her language of primordial consciousness is literal and concrete. Words are action vehicles of discharge, manipulation and invasion that ignore or destroy autonomy and boundaries between herself and others and create an undifferentiated world. It is a body and action language expressing a sense of rage and contempt for reality she is unable to express in representational language. The language is respiratory and gastrointestinal, in the service of discharge and excretion or concealment, withholding and withdrawal. Although she does not comment on it here, as a young person she was diagnosed with anorexia/bulimia. Swimming has been very important to her and she frequently endangered herself as a teen by breath holding underwater for dangerous periods of time. An example of verbal diarrhea is the "letters" she regularly mailed to multiple persons that demonstrate absence of boundaries and a sense of privacy. She made herself catatonic by withholding and literally trying to bite off her tongue so she would not have to talk.

Her mental state lacks boundaries or differentiation between inner and outer reality. She interpreted the words of others in an undifferentiated way as assaulting her insides; as prohibitions or commands to be responsible which enraged her and made her withhold. Once she flew into a rage at a landlord who ended a conversation with her by saying "Take care," because she interpreted his words as concrete coercion to do what was for her anathema. She repeatedly attacked behaviors in others that she interpreted in ways that were actually clear descriptions of how she acted, and demanded they be responsible for them. She describes her inability to integrate and represent emotions and related ideas graphically in her analysis of *Of Mice and Men.*

Caroline formed a delusional sense of self. She literally embraced her difference from others, from humankind, with a secret sense of contempt, believing, in the sense of identity (not identification) or undifferentiation with her father that had been forced on her, and then seductively encouraged by her parents' example and provision of materialistic and hedonistic gratification, that she was exempt from the rules, limits, constraints and ethics that governed others, and was entitled to enact and expect others to support her uncontrolled destructiveness and self-gratification. One of her father's maxims was "If you can't be the best of the best then be the best of the worst." Others were expected not only to live within reality and the rules, but to take total responsibility for her and take care of her, and were treated with overt or secret expressions of rage and blame when they did not live up to her double standard expectations. She did not experience this and similar double standards as contradictory, nor was she able to experience contextually appropriate feelings of guilt or shame.

Caroline does not have her own words and lives in a world of her own creation, that has no connection with consensual reality, as a means of avoiding the threat and responsibility that accompanies awareness of being alone and needing to take initiative in a world of separate persons. Mature language represents an integrated responsible self in a differentiated world where people are separate individuals. It requires touching others and being touched. This commitment and having to be aware of and bear emotions takes too much work and makes her too vulnerable. Instead she uses words and language as a way to create a secret idiosyncratic world where she cannot be touched.

How did this come about? Incidentally, professional contacts with parents during her hospitalization generally corroborated Caroline's impressions of her parents as she was eventually able to articulate them to me many years later. Caroline describes vividly how she and her mother never attached physically, emotionally or verbally and yet they were merged in an undifferentiated state of passivity, spending much of their time in mother's bed, projecting their minds onto TV sitcoms. They never bonded and never separated. Mother used words to escape contact and responsibility and to recruit Caroline into a regressed catatonic state; taking her to bed until puberty when Caroline finally objected, and actually urging Caroline to escape from the hospital during one outing they were permitted together. Mother's language neither reflected accurate perception and support of Caroline's innate characteristics and potential strengths, of which we gradually and piecemeal learned over the course of many years, nor was it intended not to communicate, but rather to discharge, manipulate and control.

Father was literally a walking bomb. He used words and language to discharge rage. He was either absent or dangerous; so threatening and assaultive that Caroline, who had not been taught self-expressive language by her mother, could not separate from him sufficiently to find words to represent emotions and related ideas about him and form a separate sense of self. Instead his identity was forced upon her and cemented with materialistic and hedonistic bribery and she took on his contempt for control, license to act and discharge rage heedless of others, and entitlement to live a life based on irresponsibility and hedonism. Among other things, his own aberrant use of language was pushed into her mind and became justification for her own destructive behavior. She would often parrot his favorite sayings, for example "You can either be the worst of the best or the best of the worst." Linguistically this exemplifies tolerance of contradiction, and condensation of destruction and destruction as construction.

Chapter 14
Jane

Jane was in her early 40s when she came to see me. She was delusional, on the verge of killing herself, isolated and withdrawn. Over the course of our many years of work she developed a meaningful satisfying life of accomplishment limited by her inability to integrate and consolidate a somatic-emotional-psychological sense of self stable enough to support and sustain herself in a close relationship. When she was in graduate school this unusually intelligent and attractive woman had been hospitalized and diagnosed psychotic with delusions, hallucinations and serious suicidal ideation. She had been devastated by the realization that the fantasy that had sustained her, that academic recognition of her exceptional mind and accomplishments in her chosen field, that involved expertise on human behavior, would fill a psychosomatic feeling of emptiness and make her feel better, was not going to come true. The emptiness, we eventually discovered, was because she completely and concretely denied having a body and emotions.

In the years subsequent to her graduate school hospitalization she had a number of therapeutic experiences all of which, judging from her subsequent accounts, failed because the therapists were either afraid of what might happen if they probed the depths of her mind and feelings, or believed the best that could be hoped for was some sort of life adjustment to her concretely perceived illness. Nonetheless, she was somehow able to return to school, graduate with distinction, and embark on what from the outside seemed an unusually successful academic and professional career. She was eventually referred to me by a colleague while in the throes of a severe regressive episode in which she isolated herself in her apartment, her hygiene deteriorated, she did not eat or take out trash, and engaged in physically self-destructive behavior.

In our initial sessions Jane believed I was about to take a knife from my drawer, assault and kill her. I had to leave the door to my office open and assure her she was welcome to leave at any time before she would agree to talk with me. She had hoarded pills and was more or less convinced she should kill herself and alleviate her pain, and repeatedly led me to think she was about to do so. She engaged in a number of overtly destructive physical behaviors. A subtle arrogant quality, her investment in the belief she was smarter than just about anyone else, something she had undeniable evidence to support, along with the extent to which she was initially threatened by my presence, led me to realize reasoning with her would be of no use. I knew that she did not have the resources to support the kind of hospital treatment she needed, and that she would stop seeing me if I suggested it. So I decided to take the real risk that she might kill herself before we could establish an alliance. She thoroughly rationalized her self-destructive behaviors and suicidal plans with the idea she knew better than anyone else what was good for her. It utterly shocked her when after we had built enough of a trusting relationship I ventured to say to her that she didn't know how to take care of herself.

One of the most remarkable things I discovered about Jane was the lack of integration of her psyche. On the one hand she taught others, conducted successful research and wrote a publication on human behavior that was widely acclaimed and valued. On the other, as we got to know how her mind worked, she did not believe any of her sophisticated knowledge applied to her personally. One of her most striking delusions was that if she shot herself in the head a beautiful flower garden would grow there. Beneath that was an even stranger idea that she had harbored since a vow she could remember making in early adolescence, namely that she literally had no body, and that she would henceforth have no feelings or care about anyone else. She could actually look in the mirror and not see anything except her head, and consistent with that she had science fiction-like fantasies and beliefs she was a disembodied head. Naturally she was uncoordinated and accident prone as a result.

As time passed her paranoid attitudes did not vanish but were more subtle and more readily identified as undifferentiated misidentifications of who was thinking/doing what to whom. I learned some shocking things about her history which were difficult for both of us to believe at first but were reiterated and acted out in the transference from so many different perspectives that we reached some certainty about their truth. Her mother had denied at birth that Jane was her child, insisting the nursery had switched the babies. She could hardly learn Jane's name and kept calling her by other names and denying their relationship. She told Jane she was ugly and never to smile because of how bad it made her look, although photos Jane showed me revealed a cute little girl. She took very poor care of Jane physically, did not tend to her when she was seriously hurt, for example when she had an avulsion fracture of her arm, and did not teach her daughter elementary hygiene. In perverse compensation for her neglect of Jane mother fed her candy, coffee, and other sweets in late evenings they spent together and Jane became habituated to such things as a way of filling the emptiness she felt inside as well as blotting out the somatic precursors of terror and rage she lived with constantly.

Perhaps her mother's most egregious neglect was overlooking her father's repeated sexual assaults on her from early childhood until puberty, something Jane remained amnesic about during our first several years of work, but gradually came to reflective awareness in the form of such things as transference fantasy that I was about to assault her, and physical behavior such as nervously rubbing her wrists and putting her elbows out in front of her face when stressed. With increasing conviction and reconstructive description it emerged that he had regularly come into her bedroom at night, tied her wrists to the bedposts, and sexually molested her. During the daytime father would treat Jane like a buddy. In place of reality Jane constructed a delusion that kept her awake at night, namely that her dead uncle was hiding in her closet waiting to spring out at her.

In her adult life despite unusual professional success Jane was unable to establish intimacy with another person. Her best friends were women who were self-destructive like her, especially one with whom she talked much of the time about suicide who eventually killed herself. So Jane created around herself a solipsistic destructive world reminiscent to me of her childhood, which reinforced her self-destructive attitudes and behaviors, her abysmal self-esteem, and provided no realistic feedback. As we learned more about these horrors and more, Jane came to think of herself as having been a feral or autistic child.

Jane's language essay

In the strange setting in which I grew up I became a wordsmith, like my father. I developed a split relationship to language. On the one hand I developed advanced skills in vocabulary and writing, and on the other hand never used language to express myself or to be known. My use of language in writing became more and more sophisticated, with language being more of an art form, or a way of expressing specialized information. I could list 50 words expressing feelings, but had no inclination to be known and be able to express my own feelings in language. I find this division between "personal" and "professional" use of language frustrating. It is frustrating when I simply can't understand you [Dr. R] or express myself. Although I am fine understanding spoken directions, etc., I am sometimes clueless about what people are talking about when they focus on the personal; their experience or mine. Basically, when I entered adulthood, I only acknowledged two broad categories of emotion – good and bad – and even then I ignored lots within those two categories or just didn't differentiate them. I had little sense of my own body; just as my mother could look at me and not see me, I could look in the mirror and not see myself and, indeed, be startled at times. It is not that I was completely ignorant. I had an extensive and well-educated vocabulary when it came to body and emotions and could use them in writing or as I talked to someone else. Their meaning, though, was not fundamentally grounded in my own past or current experience.

What I relied on to know (or, to guess, I should say), was the non-verbal – the sneers, laughs, grimaces, tone of voice, stomping away, silence, etc. And the touching, throwing, intrusion. My sensitivity to language as the material of art, and to gesture, has been useful occupationally. But left me without any inclination, or even understanding of what it meant to truly relate through language, which is where you met me. There was my focus on your gestures and obliviousness to my own. I can remember saying, again and again, some version of "That's just words."

When I think of language/communication in my family, I am struck with how unbelievable everyone's statements were, including my own (though I didn't know that at the time). Although both my parents had extensive vocabularies (both read multiple books per week) and prided themselves for proper pronunciation and spelling, they seemed to use language in solely an instrumental way or superficially gossipy way or emotionally explosive way or not at all. I have virtually no sense of learning anything about myself or anyone else by virtue of verbal labeling or explanation or demonstrating similarities between me and a family member.

As you know, my mother routinely called me by the wrong name – generally the name of the girl who lived next door and, sometimes, by my grandmother's name. The names were nothing alike. Similarly, my aunt who lived with my nuclear family called me by various other girls' names, including that of her sisters. When I was in college, I announced (in a rare assertive move) that I wasn't going to answer to the wrong name, and, indeed, when my mother or aunt called me Gail or Mary or whatever I did not respond at all. This precipitated one of the few angry exchanges between me and mother/aunt, where I was condemned for being snotty in refusing to answer when I *knew* they meant me.

As well, my mother at times didn't quite recognize me. For example, at one point I started wearing contact lenses after wearing glasses for over a decade. She didn't say anything. When I mentioned the change in my appearance, she exclaimed "I can't even recognize you without your glasses!" But, moments before, she hadn't recognized that I didn't have my glasses on! When I was 6 or 7 a neighbor took a photo of me and when my mother looked at it she exclaimed, "I never noticed you were so fat!" I was not fat at all. Nor ugly, as I was later called. And, later, when I had toothaches because of large cavities, having never gone to a dentist, my mother would look in my mouth (rare for her to be willing to come close to my body) and say there was no cavity and give me an aspirin. There were large black cavities in back molars that were immediately visible.

My mother was delusional/thought-disordered/mistaken/lying most of the time so anything she said was likely to be untrue. Confronting her was useless. She would either insist that what she said was true or deny she'd said it or attack. Even when she wasn't conspicuously baffling to me and to others such as my brother and sister-in-law she seldom seemed to actually intend to communicate, or relate, in the sense of revealing herself and wishing to know the other. She would go on and on, complaining, explaining, expressing worry, and never show the slightest interest in my reaction to what she said.

My father had more capacity for and interest in actual communication, though he also lied if it sounded better to him than the truth. I remember one time when I was a teenager and he told someone something about me that wasn't true; I said later that he knew what he said wasn't true and his response was that it sounded better. At the same time, my father was very interested in words. He wrote poems and stories and liked word play and limericks.

My aunt was the most grounded in reality and in clear communication but her specialty was silence; not speaking to what was obviously true and chastising my brother and I when we said out loud what was going on. She was taken with spelling.

Words for emotions were massively limited and it was more likely that I would be called ridiculing names than that there would be any interest in the nature and cause of my emotions. UPSET was the major category of acknowledged and self-acknowledged emotion for me and NERVOUS for my mother (subsuming phobic anxiety and snarling anger and contempt) and MAD for my father. HAPPY wasn't a coin of the realm, nor LOVE, nor anything akin. I remember my mother worrying out loud one time about my brother because he was so happy to be so successful in his occupation. "How will he handle the inevitable failure?" she wondered.

I was always scanning the behavior of my parents as a means of guessing what they might be up to next.

What I know about my language acquisition is from my mother, who was not committed to truth. However I have no reason to assume her often repeated stories are wildly distorted. According to my mother I did not begin speaking until I was about 2½. Until then I used, she said, three names, but no other words. The names were for my father (*DaDa*), brother (*Barbie*, which I assume was an approximation to *brother*, not to his actual name), and great-aunt (*KayKay*. Her name was *Catherine*). I assume I acquired her name after my nuclear family moved in to live with Catherine, shortly after I turned 2. When I was an adult I asked my mother "No name for *you?*" and she said no; she did not indicate that she thought this remarkable. In one of the conversations I had with my mother, I said something like, "So I babbled but just didn't talk?" and she said that I had not babbled. My brother had, she said, but not me. All I did, she said, was cry. Constantly. At some point, maybe when I was around 2, my mother expressed concern to the pediatrician that I might be deaf or retarded. Well, obviously I wasn't deaf, and it seemed unlikely I was "retarded" since I reached other developmental milestones early. The story about toilet training, according to my mother, is that at 18 months she began finding me in the bathroom, silently waiting to have her undress me. By 3 I could manage zippers and snaps and buttons and didn't need her assistance. Around 2½ when we moved in with my great-aunt I believe that finally there was an adult who had some capacity for warmth and who paid some attention to me so I had someone to talk to. The story is that I immediately spoke in complete sentences and excellent pronunciation save for a few specific words. My readiness to talk thereafter was received with perplexity. My mother described me, at 3, with a sense of disapproval, as a "chatterbox." At any rate, that seems to have been the high point of my talking for the sake of making contact.

Since I wasn't given any words for external body parts, and since the message was clear that the body and body experience was not to be referred to or, better yet, even noticed, it is not surprising that I learned next to nothing about internal bodily feelings and, moreover, never learned to pay attention to them. I remember only the general designation "down there" for my body below my waist, and otherwise pretty much nothing. As you know, when I had my first menstrual period (having no info about it), I thought I was dying, but did not tell my mother because I feared she would be upset at having to handle my death and that my father would be angry at me for upsetting my mother. The next day, after she found my stained underpants, she greeted me at the door by asking, "What did you do in your pants?" in a cold, rigid way. I began sobbing and apologizing and saying I didn't know and she told me to stop crying – that that was ridiculous – and to go to the bathroom and see if I "had done it again." Well, yes, of course, and I continued howling in distress, now believing that I was inadvertently soiling myself – since my mother seemed more angry and disgusted rather than worried. Again, she told me that "this" was nothing to cry about, that "it" happened to every girl, and not to tell anyone. I had no idea what "it" was or why "it" happened or the bodily basis for "it" and, moreover, given my mother's statement that "it" happened to every girl, I thought "it" happened once, so the second time was nearly as traumatic as the first. Somewhere along the line – not immediately – the word "period" was introduced but I didn't acquire any further vocabulary until I borrowed a "what to tell you daughter" book from a friend who had been given it by her mother. Certainly, I had no idea that breast development was related to menstruation, though I learned that that was bad too. My mother shoved a bra into my hands one day and told me I had to wear it – not that it fit, nicely supporting my idea that the issue was to hide.

So I must have learned that talking isn't useful. My attempts to express sadness/distress and my Aunt Catherine's refusal to speak to what she saw going on related to this attitude. Both of these led me to assert "That's just words," with a kind of world-weary, arrogant contempt. Before I met you, I knew that my gestures and body movements were noteworthy, though they were more a matter of concern to me, rather than a source of information about myself. When I was in therapy in my senior year in college, the professor who was my therapist was writing a paper on nonverbal communication. He was fascinated by my gestures, but in a way that was disruptive to the flow of communication. I would do something – wag my hands or put my hands behind my neck – and he would ask "What does THAT mean?" The flow of talking (to the extent that I maintained any flow) was interrupted by his curiosity about my gestures. Now, I am open to the possibility that I was overly sensitive and interrupted a meaningful query as a disruption; the result, though, was that I froze and tried not to move. As well, in addition to specific gestures, I also just "froze," that is, stopped and remained motionless – say, walking across the floor – when I couldn't figure out what to do next. I was concerned myself about my hand turning, or wrist turning. It seemed to me to be like the movements of autistic children and I wondered how that fit with my talking so late – which, again, made it something to try and stop, not understand.

When we first started to meet I couldn't imagine having enough to say to fill more than an hour (if that) a week. I had virtually no experience noticing and putting into words my bodily and emotional experience, no experience talking about relationship, and no expectation that I would ever put into words the vivid daydreams (and delusions) that I held. More than not being able to express myself, I also refused to give in to the expectation that I would reveal myself clearly in language. This interests me now in a way that it hasn't. So much of my life involved giving in to others' rejection, manipulation, violation of me, one NO I could silently assert was the no to expressing myself. Very sad.

I remember in particular one incident when you said something truly hurtful to me at the time you were ending your marriage. Your comment was devastating to me though I had gained enough to be able to say "That was mean," which was an accomplishment in itself. I remember at the time feeling appreciative when you acknowledged this rare meanness on your part, it confirmed in a way that you WERE trustworthy, but I also couldn't take it in. It wasn't that I wanted you to say more. I thought to myself that what you said was enough, but it just didn't touch me. You asked what else I wanted and I said I wanted you to write out your apology. And you did. And I kept that slip of paper for years. I needed the concrete, the gesture; the words/language weren't enough for me to absorb your message. As I think about this long-past incident, I know that it wasn't that I disbelieved you when you spoke, but that your statement couldn't get through to me and I needed the written out message for that. It WAS important that you were willing to do it, but that wasn't the major thing. The major thing was my inability truly to be affected by your verbal statement in itself.

Until you began showing interest in my gestures, I never thought of them as having meaning, only as showing my pathology which was being betrayed even as I tried so hard to pass as normal. Initially, I did not welcome your interest, since I felt like my gestures were "out of control" and I didn't want to acknowledge this. Gradually, I came to be able to receive your interest as, in fact, interest in me, and not an over-focus on an element. Still I felt for a long time that you were "catching" me and I was upset that I couldn't better be in control of myself. It took a very long time for me to come to want to understand myself and thus to tolerate your wanting to as well. I really hated the idea ("your" idea, I thought) that my gestures might be informative. And then I began to track when I twisted my wrists or put my hands on my neck, etc. (and also when I "froze" at home) and realized that my gestures emerged when I was particularly anxious or threatened by some mental state (whether memory and/or emotion). I began to have a sense, or to accept your view, that different gestures had specific meanings – and so I began to have a sense that the wrist turning was related to being tied, or held down, for example and to be aware that from an early age my father was silently molesting me, and there was no language for what he was doing or for how it affected me emotionally or bodily. As I've become more aware of my past experience and present states, and better use of language, my gestures have decreased in prominence.

Now, about my attention to your gestures. My response to you was exactly what I accused you of. I pounced on any observation of your movement and attributed a BIG meaning, usually sexual and a matter of your self-preoccupation. It wasn't just that I thought that your touching your tie was a substitute for masturbation; it was that I thought it *outrageous* that you would do it and think it ok. Thus began what has emerged as a conflict (never know if I am using that term rightly) between my anger about the freedom you gave yourself and my wish to be able to give myself the same freedom. Basically, I don't think there were any "neutral" movements that were possible for you to engage in – everything was fraught with sexual meaning which meant that you were dangerous to me (to the extent you knew what you were doing) or mentally clueless (and thus also dangerous, but not intentionally so). Or, incredibly self-centered and preoccupied with your own concerns (as in, putting cream on your hands[1]). Sigh.

Discussion

Jane's language of primordial consciousness is instrumental; a concrete object or thing to be manipulated for particular purposes such as a craft or profession, at which she was unusually successful, or to convey her false self. She was not able to represent emotions and related ideas and had no words for body parts and sensations. She "lived" in a gastrointestinal world of eating and excreting, and a world of body gestures whose meaning she had no words to describe. She used words that ostensibly referred to my mood, thoughts and behavior but were undifferentiated statements of her own; a stimulus bound focus and distractibility that included anger at me when I would introduce into our conversation thoughts she had previously expressed that related to things she was currently talking about but were not integrated in her awareness. She was often so concrete that when I mistook her references as metaphors or symbols she became confused and angry, despite the fact that in her working life her vocabulary was unusually sophisticated.

What can be inferred about the particular content of Jane's primordial conscious language in relation to what happened during the attachment phase? Her parents did not use language to represent and communicate their thoughts and feelings. Mother believed the baby that was presented to her at the hospital was not her own, and for the most part she did not recognize Jane by name or comment about her with accurate bodily and emotional perception, hence from the start Jane's language was not connected with recognizable aspects of herself. When Jane made efforts to communicate with mother about tangible aspects of reality mother often ridiculed her or said she was lying. Jane's father seemed to know her as a companion during the daytime but from an early age molested her at night and taught her silence, suppression and either rejection or fantastic childish mis-labeling of her bodily responses. These included the belief she had two separate circulatory systems, and a magical undifferentiated belief that the sexual excitement that had been stimulated in her prematurely was the cause of her father's behavior. Language was employed by her parents to conceal or to concretely express hostility. Both parents expressed meaning in gesture and action. The other significant adult, her aunt, conveyed the message that reality was not to be represented verbally. The fact this very intelligent woman did not talk until age 2½ and then suddenly in full sentences reflects absence of a primordial consciousness language based self and the dissociation between language and her bodily and emotional experience.

As Jane could not recognize her body or represent somatic and emotional states and could not convey essential thoughts and emotional states in language, her sense of herself was delusional. In early puberty she recalls making a vow not to feel and not to need or care about other people. Mother fed her candy and other sweets, and it seems that Jane fused with mother's hatred of her and in her vow took on mother's attitude as a form of self-control, and the sweets as concrete filling of the emptiness she felt related to absence of a somatic-emotional sense of self. She recalls practicing not feeling and not recognizing her body and when I met her it gradually emerged she did not believe she had a body. She told me when she looked in the mirror she did not see anything. As a result she was accident prone, as well as engaging in physically destructive actions with seeming unconcern. She identified herself with science fiction images of disembodied heads. She was seriously suicidal not for the usual reasons but because she believed she knew better how to live than anyone else. One of her active delusions involving contradictory meanings was the belief that if she were to shoot herself in the head then a flower garden would grow there. Had she access to guns I think she might have shot herself. Her experience both expressive and receptive remained somatically encoded in the form of action, gestures and expressions. These were often associated with hostile images. These actions and perceptions were repetitive; frozen in time; not fantasy or memory or current reality. Jane used the undifferentiated language of primordial consciousness to remain in a merged passive self-destructive identity (not identification) with her mother and avoid the work of caring for herself and making active caring relationships with others.

Notes

1 It's been a long time since I wore a tie while working. However, in the winter when the humidity was very low and my hands were very dry I would sometimes put hand cream on while talking.

Chapter 15

Charles

Charles was in his late twenties when he consulted me because he was almost literally immobilized by a sense of despair and hopelessness in a world he believed to be hostile and dangerous. He was seriously contemplating suicide. He had broken off a therapy that was based primarily on medication and had not been effective and, little did I know the irony, wanted to try therapy based on talking and understanding. We worked together for many years, as much as anything else on the subject of his reflexive withholding and refusal to talk and its relationship to his inarticulate global rage and intolerable despair.

Charles was reclusive and withdrawn. He had one "friend," who as it gradually emerged, used him in various ways including financially, borrowing money and not repaying it. Charles had inherited a fortune after his father's suicide so that he did not need to work, although he was by no means lazy. He spent much of his time in the basement of his apartment, taking apart, cleaning, and rebuilding his precious motorcycle. This ability turned out to be a precursor of one of the strengths that he was able to develop over the years, a remarkable capacity to make or repair almost anything in the nonhuman sphere, from houses and furniture to sophisticated electrical and electronic gear.

Not long after Charles and I commenced meeting he got drunk one night and held a shotgun to his head, but at the last minute he decided to call me and ask for help. For years our relationship was characterized by prolonged silences during which he would breathe audibly and rhythmically through his mouth in an almost snorting manner that reminded me of a steam engine, while darting glances at me and then looking away. In this hypnotic or mind-deadening atmosphere I had all I could do to remain awake and focused. I gradually realized that he was trying to destroy my mind and make me withdraw into a mindless sleep-like state similar to what he had done during his early years. When I would ask him for his thoughts he would claim his mind was blank. Although we gradually discovered his modus operandi was psychically annihilating others by withholding, and shutting down his mind as well – at one point in response to his associations I said he was trying to be a stone in a Buddhist garden – it turned out that indeed he did not have formed thoughts, as his experience consisted almost entirely of somatic tension and turmoil sensations in various parts of his body along with sadomasochistic mental images like chopping wood or chopping himself to pieces, that for a long time he had no words to express. Very gradually a sense that the world was a terrible place filled with hostile people as well as an overwhelming sense of rage for which he had no words emerged along with the undifferentiated sense that my efforts to pay attention to him and encourage him to talk were attacks or criticisms.

Charles's childhood had been spent in relative isolation in the country home of his wealthy upper class parents and their servants. His mother was an out of control, probably psychotic alcoholic whose daily routine consisted of getting drunk, verbally and sometimes physically assaulting Charles's father when he was present, and then at night prowling the halls of their house, banging on the locked door of the separate bedroom of Charles's father, and then alternately invading the bedrooms of Charles or his older brother. She would crawl into bed with Charles and rain name calling assaults down on him while telling him how special he was and pleading for his love. He would try his best not to move, to withdraw and shut down his mind, like an animal playing dead, and eventually she would roll over facing away from him and fall into a drunken stupor, often with her nightgown hiked up so that Charles was confronted with her naked rear end. In the morning the kitchen and bathroom would stink of vomit and diarrhea, and while mother slept it off Charles would try his best to clean up the mess, get her some breakfast, and get ready for school.

Father was in his own way as reclusive and withdrawn as Charles turned out to be. He commuted to work where he was the CEO of the successful multigenerational family business and when at home and not locked in his bedroom he spent much time in his own separate house on the family estate, characteristically walking off in the evening during mother's tirades and leaving Charles and his brother to their mother's mercy. He did make some efforts to get good schooling for his son and encourage him in that area as well as in sports, but Charles barely got by at school and his increasing withdrawal and problems reading and writing were understood to be the product of a learning disability. Around the time Charles entered puberty father was hospitalized at a psychiatric sanitarium. He was eventually discharged and, it seemed in retrospect, came home to die. He took to his bed where he would spend the days more or less immobilized. When Charles was in his early teens father shot himself in the head with a pistol, leaving Charles with his mother.

During the many difficult years of our work Charles gradually gained the ability to think and to use language to reflect his thoughts: abilities he was convinced he did not have prior to therapy. He was able gradually to transform his somatic experiences and visual images into thoughts and feelings that were differentiated from his percepts of the external world and to become aware of his emotions, principally an enormous rage and intolerable despair. His initial aspiration as he realized how enraged he was, was to become the world's most angry man. Charles's split mind consisted of overwhelming rage, hatred, fear and despair along with the belief that would emerge during periods of grievance that he deserved restitution or compensation from the world/me in the form of someone transforming things so that all the hurts of his childhood would never have happened. Much as he complained about being his mother's victim he kept reliving the affects, body sensations and mind-set, both in his mental states and in relationships with women. With women he would be sexually aggressive, discharging his anger, but not overtly sadistic, and would be secretive about the details of the relationship, not wanting me to know. As it turned out he was clinging on to the special relationship he believed he had had with his mother that excluded his father.

As a result of our many years of work he slowly developed a sense of being a separate person with an incredibly painful past and opportunities for constructive action in the present and future. It turned out he tended to pick women with their own unconscious senses of grievance, deprivation and anger and get entangled in webs of mutually undifferentiated hostility and withdrawal. He married and with much therapeutic help he and his wife were able to adopt a child of another ethnicity. He began to develop his first love, based on the desire to nurture and protect a child who was at first not well differentiated from his deeply injured self, from the kind of pain he had experienced. This motivation gradually developed into an occupational identity involving work to provide opportunities for underprivileged children. It turned out that far from being mentally disabled he became an avid reader and good writer. He began to demonstrate considerable artistic talent along with other abilities. He went to art school and eventually his work was displayed at a major museum, but he gave it up when we realized the making of it was regressive in so far as he worked in a darkened room creating a hypnotic experience using repetitive images taken from old family photographs, often of women swimming or dancing. After a time away from art that involved productive work in his therapy he gradually returned to work in entirely different media with content that was light, colorful, and much more human, although he mostly kept his work private and did not exhibit it.

Charles's language essay

As I try to think about when I first began to speak and use language what comes to my mind are a jumble of images. These images are of particular recurring events in my childhood: my mother as she prowled the house in nocturnal drunkenness giving vent to the hatred and rage that had taken up residence in her heart[1]. My father barricaded in his room behind a closed door so resolutely shut that even his breath was hopelessly imprisoned. My brother and I in our beds in separate rooms, on the one hand sharing in a common experience, while on the other hand, isolated in an every-man-for-himself numbed terror. Our mother leaving off her battering ram assault on my father's door, turning and heading down the hall to perform for us, her defenseless awaiting audience. The pounding and yelling that had had no effect on the solidity of my father's door. The shock waves of its percussion not traveling through the dead stillness of the air within.

These and many other scenes like them recurred regularly during the course of my childhood and, I believe, began in my infancy. The mechanics of language use I acquired in the course of my childhood. Although, what I had learned was exhibited as learning disability in my early formal education. Little did I know that learning required a desire to know. What I needed to know was unsustainable for me in the situation I was in. What I needed to know was that I existed in a world which had no love in it. It would have required a caring adult in my personal life and less of a desire on my part to conceal myself in the presence of others.

The uses for language were based in the fact that language was being used both as a weapon with which to attack others and as something that could be withheld. Speech could be denied and in so doing be used to reject another person. Even more powerfully, withholding could be used to annihilate the very existence of another person.

My ongoing struggle as an adult has been to find the words to speak about these events and, primarily, to construct a mental space adequate enough to hold my feeling in the form thought and memory of past events. My emotional responses to childhood events have an ever present quality to them. I have felt them as if they were in the moment and am prone to having emotional reactions to current events based on them. The possibility for my having an experience that was "new" did not exist for me for a long time. Unarticulated and undefined feelings have held a numbing sway over the course of my life.

What it means to me to really "use" language is to have in my own possession the ability to create meaning out of my experiences. With such a tool I have begun the process of speaking to myself and in so doing I have slowly been gaining the ability to think. The first level of knowing I have been confronted with has been to acknowledge the facts of how I was treated as a child. To make a distinction between what I wished to be true from what was actually the case. I wanted to believe that my mother loved me even when the way I was treated had no love in it. The second level of knowing has involved coming to know what I did, how I altered reality to fit the need for self-preservation in the face of mistreatment. One of my most painful realizations has been that I have spent most of my life trying to annihilate myself and in so doing turned to hating myself and other people; others who could care to me and for whom I could care. Without such knowledge it has not been possible to have sustaining experience of myself.

I do think that the ability of language to hold all experience has its limits and can only serve as an approximation to the fullest quality of emotional experience. There are some horrors that are beyond words.

I became aware of this [the use of withholding words and language to annihilate another person] through the course of many hours spent in therapy withholding my thoughts and feeling from my therapist, shooting him suspicious dagger glances while believing he was withholding from me. Or, attempting to engage him in a cat and mouse drama trying to lure him in with an expectant look then darting away as I retreated from his attentive gaze. There we would sit as I attempted to keep him captive in a war without words. On the receiving end, being spoken to was a threat and an attack on a very fragile sense of myself that I felt I need to protect at all costs. I have had a sense of myself based on a mistaken understanding of the attributes of my feelings.

Trying to understand how my un-thought-about responses to these early experiences have entangled themselves in my adult relationships has required being able to define and identify my feelings and the beliefs I formed based on them. My reeducation in the use of language has been a big part of developing a more satisfying life. Learning to use language, to speak, to exchange words knowing that in good faith they are being delivered with a caring effort to construct a meaningful moment has been a monumental task. My laborious reeducation in the use of language has created the possibility of specifying, defining, making distinctions and constructing a contingent meaning with which to approach new experience with a greater degree of openness.

During the long course of my psychotherapy I have become aware of a process that has taken place in me involving the harsh emotional conditions that were an ongoing feature of my early childhood and how they became registered in me as my own experience and became part of me. I understand much of my core emotional makeup as having formed around feelings of frustration, fear, and rage. How much of these feelings I took directly from my mother as a physically dependent infant having no separate and independent self-existence, and how much of them I developed on my own as a response to having my needs neglected, is hard to say. It is clear to me that, before developing the ability to put words to the service of representing my actions and emotions, what I experienced was registered in my physical person as bodily sensations.

Primary to these sensations is an idea of toxicity associated in my mind with bodily fluids: stomach juices, urine, burning tears, acidic semen, and the whiskey my mother drank to give herself permission to unleash the fury that in turn consumed her. Like one of Dante's occupants of hell who in death undergoes a bodily torment that metaphorically corresponds to the sin they engaged in during life, so my mother's internal organs in the week before her death dissolved to such an extent that ruptures of her digestive and alimentary tracts caused her to regurgitate her own feces.

It has been extremely difficult for me to find direct expression in words for the intensity of rageful feelings. As physical sensation I am aware of them as a rawness of the surface of my skin, as a churning acidic sensation in my gut and at times intestinal cramping and diarrhea. As a suppression of the feelings I have experienced labored breathing, tightness of my throat, and constipation. As a young boy I remember having a sensation in the inside of my wrists and ankles that felt like itching deep under my skin. I would bite and scratch at these areas to try to stop the sensation. Although I never had the thought of slitting my wrists I have often thought after becoming aware of how angry I have been that the idea was there in some rudimentary bodily form.

For most of my early adulthood sleeping was a way to avoid becoming aware of the intensity of my feelings and to making decisions about how best to deal with them. As I have learned to bear being consciously with myself while experiencing inner moments of rage I have on occasions experienced an almost involuntary clenching of my facial muscles that drag the corners of my mouth downward, forming a forlorn infuriated grimace. When it has happened it has been an extremely disturbing experience. On the one hand I knew I was doing this, while on the other hand I felt as if it was something I could not control. It began at a time when I had become aware of being inwardly very angry but not able to communicate to anyone or even to myself fully the intensity of the feeling. At an earlier time when I had no awareness of my inner emotional life I would not have been as frightened by such an occurrence. Being in an intermediate place of knowing that my emotional state is what it is and at the same time having a somatic expression of it that feels involuntary is extremely disconcerting. Becoming aware that one is emotionally disturbed is deeply frightening though a necessary step in gaining the capacity to bear the content of one's own mind. A similar experience has been a painful ache in my chest around the solar plexus. It is a deep and awful ache. I have experienced it most acutely when first waking. It's what I imagine a prisoner might feel like who awakes on the morning of his execution. The first seconds of consciousness are peaceful as though he has experienced a moment in childhood when he had no cares and woke to enjoy the warm morning sun streaming in his window. Then, within the next second, the awful awareness of the reality of the day. When I have this physical feeling I also have coinciding self-destructive fantasies about being impaled on a wooden pole or having a spike driven through me at my core. What I have been helped to gain awareness of is that the executioner is the raging little boy of my childhood that needs my adult attention. With this help I have become better able to bring the disparate warring parts of myself to the negotiating table and learn to live under the same roof.

Discussion

Charles's language aberration was so extreme that this unusually intelligent man, who after years of therapy developed a large vocabulary and a love of reading and communicating, was believed as a child to have a learning disability and dyslexia. In the course of our work language became the way to have a mind and self; a way to hold experience; in his case experience so unbearable that it was hitherto encoded in an undifferentiated world of somatization, disconnected imagery, affectively driven action and delusional belief so concealed that he hardly had words to express it. He developed the capacity to reconstruct from these experiences memory, to communicate it to others who are differentiated from the experience and from himself, and thereby to have a sense of self in relation to others. Language has become the vehicle of reflection; speaking to himself and thereby having an identity or non-delusional sense of self.

Charles's language of primordial consciousness was concrete and instrumental or enactive. In lieu of language based on emotional/ideational representation there was gastrointestinal, urogenital and respiratory somatization of experience, destructive affect-driven images of chopping and destroying accompanying an inchoate self-hatred but without emotional awareness or reflective meaning. He lived in the moment, with a concrete sense of immediacy. Although he knew in formal language and imagery what had happened to him as a child and often talked about his mother's assaults and his father's absences, the images were not connected in terms of emotion-laden represented memories, but were often accompanied by a low level resentment toward me who encouraged him to communicate, and an undifferentiated belief I was making the experience happen and hence attacking him. Rather than a differentiated reflected-upon personal history he reenacted what the experience must have been like as though it were happening between himself and me. Charles enacted unrepresented rage by somatopsychic withholding with unarticulated intent to punish or annihilate, and by various actions, for example with his penis with women, and in therapy by making piercing gazes at me and concretely interpreting my encouragement to articulate rather than withhold his anger concretely as command to use words as weapons to act out anger toward me rather than talk about it and reflect on it. In his undifferentiated state he was filled with violent images, and burning somatic sensations in his gut. He sought out women with big breasts that he imagined would give him what he lacked. He withheld mental content and directed piercing glances at me while emitting regular loud hostile breathing sounds. He perceived me and my comments as hostile and critical toward him.

Charles learned language from a mother who regularly invaded his personal space at night when drunk and mercilessly verbally attacked him while labeling what she was doing as loving him and wanting love from him in return. In their undifferentiated state she attributed her hostile, uncaring, rejecting attitude to Charles and her forceful attacks elicited in him a diffuse somatized rage he had no language to express and whose origin he could not differentiate. Invaded in an undifferentiated way by his mother's attacks, they became part of his psyche. Charles's father was largely absent, spending much time away from the family and when present withdrawing by being psychically unavailable or by literally barricading himself in his room. Charles turned his unrepresented rage on himself and did his best not to exist, especially at night when, unable to block the door to his bedroom/self the way his father did, he would deaden himself, barricade his mind and try to destroy it with the primitive belief that if he did not exist he would not be noticed by mother and she would go away.

Charles's delusional sense of self was not obvious. After some time in therapy I ventured and he accepted the idea that he experienced himself as a kind of rock in a Buddhist garden; something powerful and inanimate; so strong that he could not be affected by experience. This related to what he came to describe as self-annihilation: an extreme withdrawal or numbing of himself from any thought or emotion and a sense of becoming inanimate or nonexistent in order to cope with assault, which he experienced in a self-object undifferentiated way, for example in imagery of chopping himself and wood to pieces with an axe or in self-destructive bodily feelings and fantasies. Much later it became apparent that his "self" was based on the belief that he was owed having all his horrible experience wiped out or eliminated so that it would never have happened. Anything short of this, such as learning to identify and bear the experience, left him with a sense of rage and of being unfairly treated.

The undifferentiated state of primordial consciousness meant he was not separate from his mother. He was continually and mostly wordlessly repeating undifferentiated states of attack and defense such as must have happened in his childhood. He could not live alone because of the constant self-attacks, and he was passive and withdrawn about initiating active new experiences of caring in the world.

Notes

1 It took him a long time to be able to identify her emotions. He could report images of her actions that confused him because amidst her name-calling rants she would attribute to him causality: withholding his love from her.

Chapter 16
Lisabeth

Lisabeth was in her early forties when she consulted me. She was an attractive, intelligent, athletically skilled unmarried woman in the early stages of a rise to prominence in education. At work she was well respected and successful, but in her personal life she tended to isolate herself and was more or less paralyzed by intense anxiety bordering on panic as well as severe anhedonia. She wanted help to extricate herself from a sadomasochistic lesbian entanglement in which she acted as surrogate father figure for her partner's children. Some years previous she had been in a therapy that focused on a similar relationship that had concluded with her being told she should learn to accept that she was a lesbian.

Lisabeth did not envision more from therapy than a brief "tune up." She had diarrhea in the waiting room bathroom prior to our sessions and during them she could barely sit still much less make eye contact. She believed she had a penis. She was able to end the mutually imprisoning lesbian relationship but it gradually became apparent she was developing a similar all-consuming possessively destructive attachment to me. She was a very inquisitive perceptive person and though I believe I avoided sharing much about my personal and professional life with her as I did with others, she quickly discovered a good deal about me. She would shadow or stalk me between appointments, staring up at the window of my office, or she would drive by my house and sometimes lurk in the neighborhood watching. She had vivid sexual fantasies about me when she was alone in her apartment yet she would not talk about feelings about me during sessions, and on those instances where there might have been some natural contact with me as my office was near her workplace, she would flee in the other direction so I would not see her. She was terrified of any suggestion we might develop a relationship and literally jumped with shock when I asked her how she was feeling about me and our relationship, admonishing me, "Don't you ever do that again!"

For much of our many years together we worked to identify and gradually resolve the intensive possessive relationship she formed with me, as a transference surrogate for her mother. It was based upon the concept of a one person world and the literal belief that there was not enough personhood for two of us, so to speak. In this cosmology I had all the attributes – literally the life that she lacked – and that somehow she needed to reduce me to a possession with no outside life of my own, and consume me. She could not accept the idea that I was a separate person and not a possession, and that I had needs and satisfactions of my own outside our sessions that did not include her. Even the idea that I needed a fee for my work was difficult to accept, because I "had it all." In our sessions she received my comments either as criticisms or as a phony pretense façade of caring. She believed I was "all technique"; my so-called caring was a phony pretense, and really I did not care about her at all.

These ideas, it transpired, were based on the deeper belief that life was what I came to term a linear scale with but two extremes. Everything was measured and at a literal somatic level she believed she was excrement, something she expressed in the bathroom prior to each session. She fully believed she was worthless and that the world outside consisted of judges criticizing everything about her and finding her worthless and unlovable. On the other end of the scale these judges, and of course me, were perfect and had it all. What superficially appeared to be an extreme idealization on closer examination turned out to be rage-filled envy and the desire to reduce me to a possession and take my life away. Our work was complicated by the fact that she interpreted everything I said not as an effort to help but as criticism, exposing her inferiority, all her problems, what was wrong with her. Much of our work involved identifying all this as feelings and beliefs, not concrete facts, and connecting them to her identity with her mother as the bad, worthless problem in relation to the person whom she believed knew everything and had it all. The implication was that she never had to work to develop an identity of her own and become separate, and more concretely as it related to therapy, that she wanted to remain "my problem" as a form of perverse endless security; bad as it made her feel about herself.

While most people feel better when they feel better, she felt worse and tried her best to use her internal mother part to trash her good feelings, initiatives, accomplishments and the like as it would have to lead to "termination" of her therapy, a word that literally produced a total body-mind world-ending reaction that we discovered meant execution; the end of her world as she understood it. Her reaction was so intense and disruptive it was a long time before the word termination could even be mentioned and talked about. She tried her best to find out where I was all of the time and to control me and my actions, and she experienced a state of panic and nonexistence during separations associated with the conviction that when she was not in my sight she was no longer in my mind. During one summer separation she literally experienced her arms as having been amputated.

Lisabeth, her older brother and her mother formed an undifferentiated interdependent triad that we gradually learned was walled off from outside influence. Her parents had divorced when she was 5 and her mother did what she could to prevent her father from spending time with Lisabeth. He did not do much to oppose his ex-wife's efforts, and after he remarried and had other children mother managed to convince Lisabeth that he had another (replacement) family and was not interested in her. Mother's only subsequent relationship with a man was conducted in such a way that he never had any real contact with the family as a unit and so was not a presence in Lisabeth's life.

The closed off nature of the relationship between Lisabeth, her brother and her mother was not readily apparent because her mother's superficial charm made many people like and even admire her, and as she grew up Lisabeth acquired an effective social persona as well. Although outside her work mother did not have much of a personal life she bragged to her children about all her knowledge and presented herself to them as an omniscient godlike figure. Lisabeth subtly repelled and avoided contact with anyone who might not share her conviction that mother was almost literally a deity, and burst her bubble. Both children manifested problems growing up; brother's most obvious in tantrums and rages that persisted into adult life. Lisabeth manifested occasional acts of destructive rage that led mother to take her to a psychologist. Brother's rages were dismissed as "just who he was," and Lisabeth was told that she was angry because her father had left her and her mother, leaving mother to bear all the burden. Her brother grew up to lead an overtly reclusive life, like Lisabeth without intimate relationships, living alone in a relatively isolated rural area, and with a job far below his apparent level of ability. Mother, a mental health professional, seems to have used her clinical "interpretive" skills as a way to find something wrong with everyone. She confided this "analytic" fault-finding to Lisabeth, especially about anyone Lisabeth might begin to show interest in. At the same time she would question any of Lisabeth's strong feelings ("Why do you have a need to feel that way?") and interests. Lisabeth was apparently a depressed and isolated child who literally hid out in parts of her house or wandered out into the fields and woods near where they lived and became very involved in nature and small animals and insects, which she seemed to identify with, and liked to "capture" and take care of.

As she grew Lisabeth developed her own social façade, like that of her mother, as well as athletic skills and adventurousness based on what subsequently turned out to be dangerous risk-taking based on not valuing taking care of her body, and a belief, which was based on fact, that she could do most physical and mechanical things better than most men. As she was attractive and intelligent, despite believing she was ugly, she received much attention and interest from men, from whom she uniformly fled in fear. Until some time had passed in our therapy she continued to idolize both her mother and her brother, and despite her increasing accomplishment and involvement in the world treated them as her best and only friends. In one of our first few sessions Lisabeth compared my appearance unfavorably with that of her brother, whom she spoke about as though he were her lover. Following any foray into the world she would call or visit her mother, who in her own grave interpretive way would raise questions and doubts about what Lisabeth had done and thereby simultaneously undercut Lisabeth's independence while reinforcing the unconscious part of Lisabeth that had no intention of separating from her family.

As time passed I learned she would regularly and selectively tell her mother things I had said to her in such a context as to provoke mother's raised eyebrow comments and subtle questionings as to whether I was behaving inappropriately and Lisabeth, gullible, was swallowing my seductions because she did not know enough to protest. As Lisabeth began to realize for the first time that she had a problem with her mother she asked if I would meet with them and help her talk to her mother, and I agreed. We had several sessions and what was remarkable was mother's conviction she knew what Lisabeth was thinking and feeling without having to inquire. During one such interchange mother "interpreted" that Lisabeth was crying because she was upset about all her problems. When I asked Lisabeth about this she vehemently denied it and said they were tears of relief that I was the first person who had ever intervened and questioned her family system.

Over the years we worked on helping her sit still, relate to me, identify and bear her painful emotions, primarily rage and fear, and seek to understand their origins, and as our relationship evolved, to recognize and bear her loving and sexual feelings. We worked on her abysmal lack of self-worth, originally expressed somatically and literally by cramps and diarrhea, and to reflect upon it as an idea or belief she had learned rather than a concrete fact. She began to identify and attempt to value her own real feelings and interests. Her successful career and the extent to which she was valued and even loved by those she helped meant little to her until well along in our work as it was based on what to her was a façade. She lived in constant terror as her accomplishments originated from a psychological attitude of compliance with those she perceived as the judges at the top end of her linear scale, and her undifferentiated paranoid certainty that if "they" learned anything personal about her they would find out that she was excrement. So she was never able to let anyone really get to know her.

She gradually developed into a rather remarkable woman, with many friends who valued her highly. Her unusual sensory-perceptual capacities that had been used for spying and possessiveness in the service of regression and lack of separateness evolved into curiosity about all sorts of things that led to expanding interests in and knowledge about many areas, as well as the basis for a secondary career as an artist. As we worked on her fear and self-attack about experiencing any intense emotion and her identification with mother's dictum that what were objectively her independent emotions were concretely her excremental identity she gradually became an unusually emotionally expressive and caring person. In her older age she was finally willing to separate from me sufficiently to try to get to know other men. Eventually she got married, but the relationship was formed out of her belief that her husband was a superior being, at the apex of the measurement scale on which she was the bottom, and that he was only attracted to her because she was fooling him. She withheld much about herself believing that if he got to know her he would despise and reject her. This led her to squash many of her own thoughts and feelings and overlook his problems so that as she became increasingly able to value her own mind she saw his limitations more clearly, spoke up for herself more, and the relationship became more overtly difficult but more meaningful as well.

Lisabeth's language essay

When I began therapy I was unaware that I was inseparable from my mother and that she had used words and dogma to teach me a concealed way of thinking about relationships and attachments. I had been "trained" and subsequently participated in a cult-like family belief system where my mother was "God" and caring is a possessive, fused state, where all are to think alike, never separate or have individual agendas. It is through this lens that I saw the world and where certain words took on alternative meanings.

I appeared on the outside to be self-possessed, articulate, competent, caring and intelligent. I fooled myself into thinking I was separate and independent by moving out-of-state after college and over the years becoming increasingly successful professionally. This was my face to the outside world. I had an operational side that spoke as if I understood individuation and all that goes with it. My hidden quest for fusion with another was invisible to me and others because I never became close enough to anyone in a non-possessive relationship for my belief system to be questioned or apparent. Inside there was a lack of insight and thought; a disconnection from and unawareness of feelings; and deep self-hatred. Well disguised were intense feelings of rage; a belief that no one could be trusted; and that any human caring was fraudulent. It was a culture of hidden doom and gloom. I was brainwashed.

I grew up in a world of words – not meaningful words; words as a way to tell me how and what to think. Words were also used as a form of presentation, disconnected from thought and emotion – yet spoken articulately using correct grammar and a sizeable vocabulary. This "educated" (but emotionally disconnected) use of language was considered one of several requirements for success – not a success grounded in self-motivation, passion, and caring, but achieved by developing a well-designed cover which, along with refined speaking, included appropriate use of other social conventions (proper handshakes, manners, and so forth). I learned my lesson well. Underneath I sought a non-thinking state of deadness.

I took what my mother said about herself coupled with her demeaning comments about me and others to elevate her to a god-like state and relegate myself to a pile of shit. Her words were truth. She would tell me how and what to think. Given my present-day knowledge about myself, I suspect her insidious intrusions into my mind were more pervasive than the exchanges I remember. Most stunning and embarrassing is that my adulation of her continued into middle adulthood so that some of the exchanges recounted here took place in my 20s, 30s, and 40s; further evidence of our barbaric entanglement.

My mother was trained as a psychiatric social worker, which she touted with arrogant pride. She consistently applied a faux diagnosis to everyone (not faux to me at the time). No one was exempt. She, however, remained diagnosis free thereby making herself appear to me to be superior to others and to me. Topics of discussion were often about the troubles or "diagnoses" of others. I, too, was diagnosed: mean, hateful, uncaring, selfish, accident prone, don't like people, angry (that was the killer – oh to be angry; the worst of sins). When I expressed anger, her favorite rejoinder was "Why do you have a need to be angry?" This was not a gentle inquiry, it was a strong put-down; a diagnosis that I was "bad" or "sick" for having angry feelings. I have come to think she believed, and taught me, that the principal human afflictions were having feelings, being autonomous, thinking differently, and caring about anyone else but her. In her way of thinking, the overarching human disease must have been "being alive." What she taught me was to value deadness and entropy although I was seen as an energetic doer, as was she.

My mother also elevated herself through descriptions of her childhood. She made herself sound exceptional. She was home-schooled through third grade and her work supposedly included reading "the classics," whatever that meant in the early grades. To me as a young child it was more evidence of her exceptionalism, as was her description of what happened when the other children got out of school. My mother's school day ended too and she was allowed to go out to play where she reportedly organized backyard drama productions with the other children, assigning them parts etc. Again, her descriptions sounded as if she were special.

My mother repeated often that she knew five languages. She noted endlessly that in college she had majored in Greek and Latin and had earned the highest score on the Greek final exam. With no explanation about content or meaning she would launch into a recitation of lines from the *Iliad* in Greek or from the *Aeneid* in Latin. To me as a little girl, she was speaking in an unknown and elevated language. Perhaps like speaking in tongues – having no comprehensible meaning yet a special connection to some higher force. Her recitations were evidence that she was a god so when she instructed me on how and what to think it was the gospel – the Truth. She had it all. I needed to get "it."

Her comments about her divorce from my father also conveyed a subtle lesson that no one ever separates and that feelings are unacceptable. Every year on the anniversary of their marriage she would say, "Oh, today we would have been married xx years," almost as if he were still there. Likewise, each year on the anniversary of his leaving she would say, "Today your father has been gone xx years."

Many times she would tell my sibling and me that my father had difficulty making up his mind to leave her because he loved both my mother and the other woman, and that my mother and father "had a wonderful relationship," that they never fought, but that his head had been easily turned. She also proudly stated that when he left she did not take a single day off from work. Goodie for her – no feelings that would require her to spend time feeling or thinking. On the one hand, it seems she was working hard to present my father as having never left her – certainly not because he cared about another woman – describing her divorce as absent of any contention or negative feelings where all was wonderful. On the other hand, for a period of time after he left we would observe her crying – confusing.

At one point after my father departed (I was five), I feebly expressed a wish to see him (other than "feeble" would have been dangerous). I remember the response: "He has another family now." I heard this as, "He does not care about you anymore." He in fact had three stepdaughters in his new marriage and my mother was "teaching" me that he could no longer care about me too and that I was not to care about him. As part of her agreement with my father he was not to introduce me or my sibling to his new family (amazing that he agreed to this – another story). As an adult, I asked my mother about this proviso. Her reason: It would have "upset" me. Wow, I might have had feelings – perhaps have enjoyed his new family – threatening to the cult. However, because of her many negative statements about his new family I continued well into adulthood to view them as a bunch of undesirables.

Becoming attached to people outside the family was subtly discouraged. When I mentioned how much I admired a certain friend my mother said, "I am watching that relationship." The implication was that the relationship bore watching because there was something wrong with my feelings about the other person, with the person herself, and with me. I was sick. Caring was forbidden. Often, when my mother met someone for the first time or when talking about a friend of mine or hers she would make a comment in a supercilious tone that so and so is "very disturbed" or "very angry" with the word "very" emphasized. I never understood what she meant by "disturbed" nor did I ask, but I think now that the categorization meant the person was a pariah. When she labeled a person as "angry" it meant that both the person and the feelings were unacceptable. She was teaching me that being angry was an intolerable human emotion yet we were tied together by anger: deep anger at each other and at any threat of leaving the cult. Her message was: "Stick only with me, your mother. Everyone else is dangerous." Indeed, I stuck.

In my 20s when in graduate school I called my mother to say I needed some help and wanted to see a therapist. Could she recommend someone? Her response: "I must have failed as a mother." No concern about me. It was all about her. I tried to assure her she had not failed (I served as her ardent apologist). And of course I heard in her comment that it was I who had failed. In retrospect I wonder, did she think she had failed because I was expressing some emotional needs? Or that I needed help from someone other than her? Both were threats to the family system. I did not tell her why I wanted therapy. I was concerned because I had become attached to another woman. I was afraid that perhaps I was homosexual, in my mind, a sickness. When I think about this now I can see that I was sick in a different sense. I was having strong feelings and given how I had been instructed, strong feelings were a sickness. I think now that I saw the "therapist" as a stand-in for my mother so he/she would either get rid of my feelings or tell me they were acceptable. Given my lack of a separate identity from my mother I was unable to make my own assessment or even find a therapist on my own[1].

When I told my mother that I was going to begin therapy [with Dr. Robbins, two decades later, in her early 40s] she responded, "Don't be too dependent; remember your heritage." In retrospect a stunner, although I had no clue at the time. In that one statement she said it all: don't leave me; don't care about anyone else; remember how I have trained you. At the time I was unaware that her comment fed my tightly held mother-crafted belief system that I was never to leave her or care about anyone else. Since I had prided myself on being "independent" (unaware I was totally tied to her) I thought "too dependent" and "heritage" was a reference to our deep family roots, which she glorified: a stereotype that we are reserved, well-educated, independent, and somewhat cool and aloof.

Early on in therapy Dr. Robbins noted that for the work to be successful I would need to form an intimate relationship with him[2]. I was shocked, puzzled, and pleased – what did he mean? Sex? At the time I was in a relationship with another woman which unknowingly filled my definition of intimate: possession and fusion. Ironically, I sought therapy in part because I thought I wanted to get away from that relationship, yet unknowingly possession and fusion was all I knew and all I that I wanted. It was my understanding of love and caring. When I told my mother what he had said (was I trying to get confirmation that there was something wrong here?; reinforce the belief system?; create suspicion?; threaten her?; or a confused mix of all?), her reply was a succinct, disdainful, "That is hard to do." Then she went on to describe how she had handled a long-ago client's expression of caring about her. Reportedly she said to the client, "My husband would be pleased to hear that." I was deeply discomforted. Even then I thought it a terrible thing to say and felt embarrassed. I was aware how devastated I would be if Dr. Robbins said something like that to me. I see now that she was instructing me (and I was buying) that any expression of caring about a therapist was unacceptable, "bad" or "sick."

At one point I found a fossil that looked a bit like a penis. My mother was walking with me and I said I would like to show it to Dr. Robbins, chuckling about its resemblance to a penis. Her reply: "You don't have that kind of relationship with him." Oops, I was bad; I should not care. It was not until many years later that I realized, and became enraged, that she was instructing me on the nature of my therapeutic relationship about which she knew little.

During one summer's separation, I was struggling with missing him, which I fundamentally could not tolerate. Testing, I said to my mother, "I miss him." Her reply: "Oh, that's just transference. I thought you had gotten over that by now." I shriveled. I had a disease called "transference". Remarkable is that my educated self knew full well what transference is but all of that went out the window. I was bad and sick once again, as was my relationship with Dr. Robbins. In retrospect, I think at that time I was hearing what I wanted to hear: I was saved from the temptation to leave the family system.

In the early years of therapy, my mother and I met together for three sessions with Dr. Robbins. At the beginning of the first session I started to cry. She moved to hug me, which I rejected (I never could stand to have her touch me). Dr. Robbins intervened to ask her why she thought I was crying. She opined that my tears were an expression of my upset about my troubles. On that basis, she had made a move to hug me. In fact, I cried because I was moved by my feelings of caring for Dr. R. It was a powerful moment: the first time in my life that a person was present who was an alternative voice to that of my mother. The experience was a small lesson in how she thought she knew what I was thinking and feeling, and how I participated by never inquiring into her thought process or expressing feelings of my own. At times I behaved similarly with Dr. Robbins. I would interrupt him before he finished a thought believing I knew what he was going to say or insisting that a fantasy about him was an indisputable fact.

As therapy progressed I began to understand that as a result of my mother's indoctrination I lived in two mental states. One I will call "mother think." The second I will call "separate think."

Mother think is the thought process adopted full-bore from my mother's brainwashing: a mother with whom I was emotionally enmeshed as one; where the family cosmology was such that a symbiotic relationship was the only way; feelings were unacceptable; and I was no good, ugly, and worthless. People outside the family configuration were not real or trustworthy; others' perspectives (including mine) were corrected to conform to her world view. For me it was an entropic state, requiring no work or development of a personal agenda. As explained earlier, while I functioned well in the world and appeared to be my own person, I was not. I continued to be enmeshed in my mother's way of thinking – a belief system that had its own word meanings. It is a destructive and hate-filled way of thinking – hate of myself and hate of others.

Separate think is a thought process shaped by years of psychoanalytic psychotherapy where I have worked to become more separate, to care about myself, create a personal agenda and feel worthwhile. In this mental state I have a self. My identity is not defined by emotional fusion with my mother or anyone else. This is a love-filled way of thinking; love of self and love of others. In this mental state words retain their commonly understood meanings.

Unconsciously I can slip back and forth between these two modes of thought. At certain times there is a strong pull to return to mother think: the destructive, entropic, no-self, no-work state where my thinking is fused with that of my mother. At these times words take on one meaning. When I am separate and have a mind of my own they take on a different meaning. In short, the meaning switches depending on which mental state they are expressing. Consequently, when I began therapy Michael Robbins spoke a foreign language, using words whose definition we did not share. Some examples follow:

When I began therapy I was unaware that I believed love and caring meant emotional fusion: that each person is the absolute centerpiece of the other's universe, never parting. Nor was I aware that I had no identity of my own but was defined by my perceived fusion with another. In therapy I acted out of this belief system by trying to possess Dr. Robbins and would become enraged when

I could not. I would dehumanize him by complaining that he "had it all," led a "perfect" life, and enjoyed "all the love he needed." He floated on a cloud being worshiped and served by others, having no problems or difficulties. I would tell him that he did not care about me and was a fraud. I kept a journal and sometimes during separations or when there were other indications that he had a life of his own and "didn't care," I would write fantasies about ways to torture or kill him.

In reality, of course, becoming fused with and trying to possess him was a form of destruction of us both. I was unaware that in mother think neither of us is a separate person; autonomy is destroyed. As much as I wanted to possess him, there was no way I could. I struggled against the reality that he was independent. I would become enraged, so much so that at times when alone, I would return to the entropic, fearful, non-thinking and agenda-less family mental state. I think at some level I knew that love in mother think also meant loss; loss of my delusion of a fused state thereby a loss of my identity.

As therapy progressed I began to experience genuine loving feelings which I could not tolerate. They were "bad" and "unreal." I had been tricked. To eliminate any positive feelings I would trash my relationship with Dr. Robbins, holding tightly to a delusion that he had the perfect life, all the love he needed and I was a nothing. He didn't care. He was all technique. Returning to my family construct became my desired state, forgetting that it was a state of misery, self-hatred, and non-caring.

Early on, even a hint of real caring and I would try to physically distance myself from my feelings by sucking in my breath and turning my head to the side, away from myself, or I would delegitimize my feelings by engaging in delusions that "proved" he was terrible and unworthy. Over time, through Dr. Robbins's insight and a lot of hard work on both our parts, I began to develop the capacity to see that love and caring are a strong and consistent feeling of affection and respect between me and another. I began to understand that there is no such thing as a one person world, and to value having a separate identity where I create an agenda of my own. This state requires work – no entropy here.

As noted previously, my mother's frequent statement "Why do you have a need to be angry?" expressed her antipathy toward feelings of anger. They are unacceptable and must be gotten rid of. If I am angry I am "bad." When angry in mother think, my feelings are diffuse with no understanding of the cause coupled with a powerful wish to eliminate the feeling. In separate think I am able to identify why I am angry and at whom or what. It is reality based and acceptable.

I surmise that "Why do you have a need . . ." is also a statement of my mother's disapproval of basic human needs. Once I asked her if I had ever sucked my thumb. She defensively replied "Absolutely not," as if the need to suck was another disease. When I began therapy with Dr. Robbins and was alone I felt the urge to suck my thumb. I tried it a couple times to see what it felt like. I speculate that when a child if I had tried to suck my thumb my mother may have pulled it out and admonished me.

Throughout my pre-therapy life I denied that I had any needs and disparaged any glimmer of need. As therapy proceeded and I began to have genuine caring feelings I started to recognize that I actually had needs: the need for human relationships, to be loved (not possessed and consumed), to express feelings, to be heard, and encouraged to be my own person. Gradually I became aware of the deep emotional deprivation I had experienced as a child and how I had been robbed of selfhood and autonomy. I began to understand how enraged I was at my mother and to accept and embrace, rather that disparage, how needy I really was.

In mother think a person who has "problems" is "emotionally disturbed"; at the bottom of the longitudinal scale, troubled, a flawed human being. There is no recognition that all people have problems with which they struggle more or less. She never conveyed the idea that a problem is something to be worked on, understood, and perhaps solved. Instead it is a permanent undesirable flaw. Okay for others to have problems, which she never appeared to have; not okay for me yet my identity was based on being her "problem." When I began therapy I transferred this way of being to the relationship with Dr. Robbins. I wanted to be his problem. I believed that the more "disturbed" I was the more he would care about me. My identity depended on it and so did his. I would talk about "us" the patients and "them" the therapeutic community, those who had no problems and got their kicks from ours. Having problems was the ticket to this elite sanctum. If on a given day I did not feel as if I had a problem to talk about I would became intensely anxious. I feared he would kick me out.

At the same time it was imperative that I keep secret that I was seeing a therapist. Yet, when anyone I knew was in therapy I expressed understanding, giving praise and encouragement. In this case I was able to switch into separate think, while in relation to myself I remained in mother think.

It took me years to understand that dependent and independent did not mean remaining emotionally fused with someone while putting on a public face that made it look as if I was independent because I was geographically separate, could live on my own, and was successful at my work. My thinking was so entangled with my mother's that I did not understand that healthy dependency is the ability to balance intimacy and autonomy, to be able to rely on others while maintaining a strong sense of self. I had no idea that when she said to me at the beginning of therapy, "Don't be too dependent," that she actually meant don't leave me; don't care about anyone but me.

The idea that a person can only love one is also implicit in her comments about my father's new family: that he could not love them and me at the same time. Her warped view of dependency is also evident by her account after attending a psychoanalytic conference. At the conference were a husband and wife who were both therapists. My mother and I knew them (at the time I was in therapy with the wife) and she described disparagingly how the couple went to all presentations together, walked together to and from them, and sometimes held hands. I remember well the condemnation in her tone of voice when she remarked,

"They were too stuck together." She was not only expressing disapproval of their relationship, but discrediting the wife whom I was seeing. This was typical in that she often found ways to disparage people with whom I developed a seemingly close relationship. There was also the implication that a normal dependent relationship is unhealthy, so stick with mother. I am sure the last thing she wanted was for me to become attached to the female therapist. At the time I did not have the insight to suspect that her comment was probably a projection, given what must have been her delusion of fusion.

In mother think transference is a disease as illustrated by the quote cited earlier: "That's just transference. I thought you had gotten over that by now." When I shriveled from the comment I was in mother think, ready to believe I had a disease. I was becoming attached to Dr. Robbins, but, as noted earlier, her comment was in part a relief: I could stay fused with her. Becoming attached in a healthy way was threatening to me.

Over time transference, of course, was key in helping Dr. Robbins and me learn about my distorted thinking. Little did my mother know that my nascent caring feelings were not transference – they were the beginnings of separate think; of breaking the destructive bond with mother. Or did she? Perhaps at some level she did know and was threatened, thereby compelling her to disparage my feelings by her comment.

In mother think a separation means a devastating loss: death, suffocation, no life without the other. Since I was wedded to the delusion that love and caring were fusion with another, when Dr. Robbins would talk about an impending separation I became terrified. I would become enraged, attacking him verbally for his supposed desertion of me and removal of my identity. His actual absence meant he did not care, got rid of me, never thought about me. I could not bear the idea that he was a separate person, independent, and autonomous; could love multiple people. I had been taught otherwise. When he would go on summer vacation I would feel as if a limb had been amputated. It is clear now that I believed I was fused with him and could not survive. In his absence it was I who tried to destroy the relationship in ways described previously. Alternatively, I would nourish the delusion that we were fused, believing he could not wait to return to me. At the initial appointment after a separation I would either deaden my feelings or angrily attack. The reality of seeing him face to face shattered my delusion. It took time for me to even minimally reconnect.

It is not surprising that when the word termination surfaced in relation to ending therapy – the ultimate separation – it felt as if it was the end of the world. Metaphorically a trap door would open and I would feel as if I would fall into nothingness. At the same time there were occasions when I tried to prove I could be "independent" (the geographic definition) by getting rid of Dr. Robbins before he could "terminate" ("get rid of me"). I would make a lame statement about cutting back on therapy citing my reason as wanting "freedom." When pushed to define what I meant by "freedom" we discovered it, too, had a dual meaning. One was a desire to return to my family state where I did not have to think or work;

could be entropic and eliminate all responsibility that goes with a caring relationship. The second was a more normal definition involving autonomy and choice. Over time I began to experience a conflict between the family system of thinking and more normal development to which I was being pulled.

I began to internalize the commonly understood definition of separation: that it and the concomitant feelings of loss and sadness are coupled with positive reminiscences about the person and the relationship; a missing of the other and a wish to see the person, not annihilation. And I began to see that the ultimate separation – termination – is not death but an opportunity for healthy independence where I incorporate new self-knowledge, internalize Michael Robbins's voice and caring and have the freedom to make the necessary choices to craft a satisfying life of my own. Of course, I will feel sad when the relationship ends.

In order to exercise ongoing control over mother think I must work to bring to my awareness the mental state from which I am acting, speaking, or thinking. Am I acting from my mother's alternative delusional world of non-separateness, or from a world of separate think where people are truly individuated and can enjoy healthy intimacy? While I am better at this, my struggle continues.

Discussion

The formal aspects of Lisabeth's language were not only intact, but highly developed. She worked in a world where language and communication were very important. However, this language was not integrated with emotional awareness and was associated with the belief, undifferentiated from her perceptions of others, and undifferentiated from somatic experience, that she was an unwanted piece of excrement. Lisabeth's language of primordial consciousness consisted of somatization, things like diarrhea, choking sensations and a sense of physical emptiness; intense affects, mostly anxiety; and constant physical activity in an effort that did not distinguish thought from action designed to escape from having to sit with affects she did not understand and had been taught to believe were bad. Her self-other undifferentiated world was animated by judges criticizing and condemning her, and at the other extreme of the "linear scale" spectrum, images of others like me who had the perfect life, with all needs met, that she lacked, and no unpleasant feelings and sensations to bear. The images of me were concrete and came from a perception that we were a single organism in the sense that I literally had the good feeling thing and the imagined perfect life experience that she lacked, therefore that I had no needs. What seemed on the surface like idealization was actually unrepresented hatred for what I "had" that she lacked. Others of her beliefs were similarly literal and somatic. If I was out of sight I was gone. She was excrement.

She did not differentiate her mind and fantasies from her belief about the world and the attitudes of others. Certain loaded relationship words such as problems, love, caring, separation, independence and termination had contradictory meanings depending on whether she used them in the undifferentiated language of primordial consciousness with meanings learned from her mother, or eventually in reflective, representational thought. In the world of fused identity the operative activity was possession, as she believed she could not otherwise survive and literally experienced end of the world panic at the thought. Loving and caring was to her something she should not do as it was associated with a belief she was being fooled and was bad. The idea that I had a life of my own and was not totally and constantly devoted to her meant that no matter how I treated her during a therapy hour it was a façade and any words otherwise were fake, designed to conceal that I couldn't wait to be rid of her. When we were separated, in her undifferentiated state she was convinced she no longer existed in my mind and heart. She tried to do away with any caring feelings about me during separations, often working herself up into frantic states as a result. When I used the language of reflective representational thought what she "heard" was the definitions in primordial consciousness mother speak so that she experienced all the terror and rage at the idea of being a separate individual that should properly have belonged to her primary attachment experience.

The root of the lack of a language-based self seems to have been a failure of basic human attachment based on love and caring. There was no indication Lisabeth and her mother had ever formed a secure, caring bond. Lisabeth could not remember being touched or held, and there were striking memories of a sense of alienation in which she had no sense of what was going on in mother's mind and therefore not knowing how to behave around her. At times she actually performed experiments to see how mother would respond in different situations in an unsuccessful effort to find out, discovering how she could get superficial responses from mother but having no internal sense of what they might mean, as words could not be trusted. Words were not based on human attachment and caring, but had other meanings to deceive and manipulate.

The undifferentiated reality was that Lisabeth's words could not be trusted. She constructed a false self that was extraordinarily successful and concealed a self-object undifferentiated sense of basic badness and worthlessness perceived as factual judgments emanating from a world imminently passing such judgments on her. The content of Lisabeth's delusional self was based on the concretely somatized belief that she was shit, associated with the idea that there was something fundamentally wrong and bad about her very being and In her fused unseparated mentality she was convinced that if anyone got to know her beneath her professional façade they would find out who she "really" was, and would hate and reject her. These were not ideas with emotional content; they were images, concrete beliefs and associated somatic sensations and actions, not subject to examination. Reciprocally, there was the notion of others' independence, for example she could not tolerate the idea that I had a life and loves (and hates) of my own as this was equivalent to total rejection and lack of caring for her. She maintained a belief that superficially resembled idealization but in fact was dehumanization and rejection, that all my needs were satisfied and I needed nothing, not even payment of her fee.

Everything was measured on a scale and rather than seeing herself and others as separate people, the other person was perceived as perfect, with no unsatisfied needs or accomplishments, and she as nothing. Like her mother and in apparent compensation for her self-hatred and sense of worthlessness and defectiveness she related to some people in a secretly arrogant way, looking for their problems and weaknesses and having a secret sense of arrogance and superiority. These beliefs were supported in her adult life by her inability/refusal to make close separate relationships with anyone other than her mother and her only sibling (and subsequently, in the transference, with me). She knew little or nothing of her emotions and during her mother's life maintained frequent contact with her that enabled her to get subtle reminders there was something wrong with any emotion she might have or anyone outside the family she might consider getting involved with, so the beginnings of strong emotions were very threatening to her and evoked powerful self-hatred associated with a belief that there was something wrong with her.

The undifferentiated language of primordial consciousness was familiar and comfortable in the sense that she associated catastrophic end of the world meanings to words like separation and termination, and to the precursors of loving and caring feelings, which were perceived not as defining herself as a separate person but as indications that something was wrong with her. What would be experienced as exciting, liberating and pleasurable to another person aroused in her a terror of imminent annihilation. She had been taught that she had no right to have her own emotions and lead a life thoughtfully informed by them, and that any movement in that direction, any awareness of love and hate and a separate self, including the accurate language in which such feelings were expressed, was actually badness at the most concrete and somatic level, heralding imminent catastrophe. We came to understand that the catastrophe referred to the absence of an independent sustainable self should she venture out of the family system where no one had a separate identity. Therapy itself was a problem, as she defined words like "patient" and "problems" as meaning she was a lesser human being and something was wrong with her, and yet in her mind the idea of being a patient in therapy and always having problems, in relation to me as the superior therapist, was a necessary shelter against the terrifying possibility that she might have to leave therapy and lead a separate life.

Notes

1 The therapist was the wife of a colleague of mother. She essentially told Lisabeth that she was homosexual, which turns out not to have been the case. The therapist had no insight into how dependently entangled she was with her mother.
2 I blush to think that I said this, but I must have. Little did I know how much this fed into the mother transference that played such an important role in the therapy.

Chapter 17
Jacob

Jacob was about 60 years of age when he was referred to me by the local psychoanalytic institute, which he had contacted in search of another in a long series of "psychoanalyses." He was a married father of three teenage sons and manager in a large technology corporation. He complained of a sense of alienation from the world around him associated with a literal sense of coldness, as well as a long list of criticisms of his wife that was leading him to consider having an affair with another woman. Not long after we met he took early retirement and remained unemployed during most of our many years of work.

Jacob had what seemed to be a truly creative mathematical mind but he had self-destructed in his efforts to actualize this ability, early in his life, as he had done with other things he was good at such as sports and music. In his later adolescent years he was haunted by powerful images of taking a knife and stabbing his mother to death, inhibited by terror and certainty he would be executed. He was hospitalized during college after telling his father that he was afraid he was going kill someone. After a promising beginning in college he became paralyzed and self-destructive trying to actualize the delusion that he could solve a basic problem in mathematics involving dividing by zero, or as I came to think about it as I learned about his doomed efforts to create a life out of a self-object undifferentiated rage and sense of defectiveness about as extreme as any I have encountered, that he could make something out of nothing.

Despite his crippling problems Jacob was able to do well enough in the world of math-physics related technology to achieve a relatively high level managerial position in a well-known electronics corporation. He was quite successful in seducing women, with, as it turned out, insecure senses of identity and masochistic tendencies, and he had numerous relationships with women whom he tried to subjugate sexually in the guise of love. He eventually married a masochistic woman who tried to care for him and their children in the face of his constant, vicious, verbal and sexual attacks and who seemed unaware of how he was treating her. Jacob was severely hypochondriacal and preoccupied with one after another of a long string of real or imagined physical ills that he was convinced were about to kill him. He was similarly and obsessively paralyzed by powerful urges to kill people with whom he got close, including in addition to his adolescent obsession about his mother, his children, and eventually me. He told me he could barely restrain himself from pushing one of his children out of the carriage in an amusement park roller coaster.

Jacob was in therapy of one kind or another almost continuously subsequent to his psychotic episode in college, mostly with psychoanalysts, one of whom had a major international reputation for treating psychotic persons. My personal experience with Jacob along with things he told me about his relationship with his wife taught me that he seemed to know no form of dialogue other than argumentation, attack, criticism and fault-finding; associated with the belief he was under lethal identity-destroying attack from the other person, and a grandiose self-elevation accompanied by the conviction he was always "right" and knew it all. It played out as a concerted effort to take control of women. He had a curious worship of psychoanalysis, as he understood it, which he thought of as like getting an advanced degree, and meant to him having the license to "free associate," that is, vent his vicious hostility and grandiosity without restraint from the therapist, who was not supposed to say anything. His perverse conduct in therapy involved acting like he was the "analyst," demonstrating his superiority, and making "interpretive" attacks on the therapist for all his or her flaws and mistakes. He literally told the analyst who preceded me that he was not to speak, and that person, the one with an international reputation for treating psychotic persons, eventually informed Jacob that he could not continue with Jacob because Jacob's relentless attacks were stirring up personal issues of his own that disqualified him from being able to be of further help.

Jacob was crushed and uncomprehending during his initial consultation with me when I told him that I did not think psychoanalysis, as he understood it, was the best form of treatment for him and that he needed face to face contact and active dialogue. It was as though I were telling him I thought he wasn't good enough to be admitted to Harvard or Oxford. His object in our sessions seemed to be to talk nonstop, a kind of know-it-all, telling me without awareness about his grandiosity what was wrong with the various people in his life, and reciting details about his body functioning and the latest condition he was certain he was going to die from. He talked about his childhood and shared various vivid images of being attacked, rejected and humiliated by his mother, but I came to realize that he had no emotional awareness of their meaning. When I shared my understanding of their emotional meaning he attacked me for failure to understand him and claimed that his relationship with his mother had been loving. It became clear he interpreted being "interrupted" by any comment I might try to make as attacking him and trying to take over his mind and destroy him. In fact he acted like we were together so that he could "analyze" me, looking for flaws, mistakes and errors, past and present, which justified his relentless attacks on me that I gradually realized represented his efforts to destroy me as a separate person.

Over many painful years he did grow and change in some ways, but never spontaneously had anything good or caring to say about me or gave any indication he remembered anything positive or caring I had done. His homicidal urges were at times quite direct, as when he had the urge to throw acid in my face when I greeted him, or throw me downstairs as we said hello on the stair landing outside my office. Having had much experience with homicidal persons in hospital settings I often sensed he was actually close to acting. Part of his justification for his behavior, the significance of which he was totally unaware for years, was that he experienced himself as being forced, suffocated, and having to "suck up," whenever I said anything. At times he was almost literally convinced I was crazy, and literally perceived me as an inhuman monster endangering him. Nonetheless he continued seeing me without any indication of stopping, whether because however unacknowledged he was getting something positive and making related changes in his life, or because of the less apparent masochistic element in our relationship that represented enactment of his early relationship with his mother, I do not know. As one might expect, it was very difficult to remain neutral and helpful in the face of his relentless perseverative attacks, which early on in our relationship I characterized as a "kill or be killed" mentality, and when I did show signs of irritation, distancing, annoyance, whatever, it only proved his point that I was basically hostile and attacking toward him.

Although Jacob presented himself as a learned cultured man, it turned out that most of his identity was based on a grandiose self he had constructed as a know-it-all about everything, including human behavior, and as someone who did not need help from anyone. His language was solipsistic in so far as when he did change in ways I could see reflected in our work, he talked as though the insights had been totally his own. Despite the life and death seriousness of our work, the last thing he would ever do was to admit to anyone other than his wife that he was in therapy, the dependent aspect of which to him meant contemptible weakness. Beneath his grandiose omnipotent façade, however, was the truth he fought for years against knowing: that he was a frightened, enraged man who could neither maintain a train of thought about himself nor identify or bear any of his feelings; that he felt frightened of the world and powerless; and that at a reflexive somatic level he literally believed he was excrement or a disease, totally unlovable. As I mentioned, even though he was in relatively good physical health he was convinced beyond reason that he was about to die of one ailment or another. His self-hatred was so total, reflexive and somatic that he lacked even a stable self with which to contemplate it as an idea. His only undifferentiated alternative was to misperceive it in a paranoid way in a world around him he interpreted as attacking him and threatening his very survival.

Jacob's beliefs, images and related actions were deeply somatically rooted. There was an endless litany of deadly illnesses and the doctor visits they necessitated; preoccupations with his bowels and encopresis and with his penis and its state of health and functional capacity to erect and ejaculate, around which his only sense of power seemed to revolve. He was driven to masturbate on a daily basis and have intercourse whenever possible, both of which I soon realized were sadomasochistic acts. As the colloquialism goes, he literally "beat his meat" to the point of physically harming his penis. He was impelled to have frequent intercourse, the unconscious purpose seeming to be to drive the woman to orgasm which he interpreted as making her lose control. When masturbating he used pornography, and one of his favorite images was of a woman sitting on his head.

In lieu of reflective representational thought his mind functioned as a disconnected series of images, of which he had a huge store; images that were often accompanied by somatic sensations and urges to act, but were not associated with emotion related thoughts. There was a recurrent transient sensation that he had a woman's breast, associated with efforts with his hands to wipe it away, and reflexive grimaces which he soon realized were actual imitations of his mother's facial expressions, which he had literally practiced in front of a mirror during his childhood. He often felt almost to the point of belief that he had a knife in his pocket when we talked. One of his repetitive images was of me literally sitting in shit; another involved sadistically abusing my daughter. Of course these things arose at meaningful places in our interaction but he had no thoughtful reflective emotional language to describe and understand. It was a long time before he was even able and willing to report these to me, and he tended to describe them and quickly move on as though they had no significance. It became more evident as time passed that he felt impotent, enraged and that he was literally aphasic, without words, when it came to trying to speak directly from his thoughts and emotions.

Jacob's mother had insisted she loved him even as she was, from all the evidence I could accumulate, abusing him. He had an unshakeable belief it was true, and that he loved her as well, even when it was manifestly evident from his reports of his life and his behavior in the transference with me that he was incapable of loving anyone, or indeed appreciating the fact that others were trying to care about and not destroy him. While it might seem inconsistent that he had images of getting a knife and stabbing her to death during his teens, deterred only by the conviction he would be executed, these images were not accompanied by any actual comprehension he was in a rage at her; they were just mysterious troubling obsessions. Yet he presented me with innumerable vivid images from various times in his childhood, in photographic detail and clarity, of her physically controlling and invading his body with her fingers, hands, and other devices, on the pretense that he, an apparently healthy child, had a serious disease; something fundamentally wrong with him inside that she had to root out and expunge. She kept him in the house and the bathroom and bedroom with her much of the time during the day on the pretext that he was ill, and was constantly bringing doctors in to diagnose and treat him for what seem mostly to have been imaginary ailments, expressing her conviction there was something terribly wrong with him and he was about to die.

The family was wealthy and mother was attractive, and there is also evidence that in the days when doctors made house calls, and father was away at work, she seduced at least one of the doctors, psychologically if not physically. These doctors were like family friends, who visited regularly in the course of which they treated Jacob. Mother was inappropriately seductive in dress and manner with

Jacob, as well, exciting and luring him to want to get under her skirts and into her underpants and private parts where he seemed to believe the secret of the universe resided. This fixation preoccupied him at an age when most boys were out playing ball. She told him he was not to go out of the driveway, which became a therapy metaphor I used to describe his inability to separate from her. She led him to believe he had done some terrible damage to her private parts, by such things as telling him stories about the horrible episiotomy she had to endure at his birth.

Father was a physically powerful person, of some stature in the construction world as well; a rough character whose favorite way of relating to Jacob was to goose him as he went up the stairs or punch him. When father came home from work mother would recite all of Jacob's badness and transgressions during the day, and father would beat him with a belt while mother looked on, wringing her hands in apparent dismay and crying. Not long after his younger brother was born, in a rare show of defiance, Jacob packed some things and told father he was going to run away. The result of this disguised plea for caring was that father opened the door for him and said "Go ahead." When he was around the same age, perhaps 7, he was playing ball with other boys in the street. The ball bounced in front of an oncoming car and Jacob, in a combination of what he retrospectively realized was a sense of omnipotence and a wish to kill himself, dived in front of it, was hit and hospitalized for some days with a severe head injury.

At the core of Jacob's problem was malignant psychosomatic self-hatred, but it was very difficult to work with him about this, as it was effectively masked by equally malignant hatred of others that he used all his rational powers to justify, as well as a kind of grandiosity and omnipotence around which he had constructed a false self, associated with the belief that he did not need help from anyone. There was an unfortunate synergy between Jacob's malignant self-hatred based in somatic symptoms and delusional beliefs and the fact that he was in fact a basically unlikeable person because of his overt nasty sadistic behavior toward others. Moreover, as he was unable to maintain a train of thought about himself and his mind worked in images and associated somatic sensations it was difficult to communicate with him.

It took a long time for me to realize that the sadomasochistic images of his relationship with his mother that were like photographs of childhood were not accompanied by any thoughtful verbal comprehension. As a result he attacked me when I would try to interpret their meaning, as it challenged his cherished belief about his loving relationship with his mother. Indeed at times he was convinced I was crazy. He and his wife eventually divorced as it slowly became evident to them as a result of my work with Jacob that her extreme masochism matched his extreme sadism, and it was only her devotion and attempts to love him and protect their children as well as her own lack of self-worth that had sustained the marriage and kept the children from being more scarred than they were by his relentless abuse. Subsequent efforts to date women revealed his need to control and psychologically destroy anyone he was involved with because he was threatened by any sense they were separate. He interpreted their attentions and efforts to care as intentions to destroy his identity. Nonetheless, over a long period of time he was able to begin to integrate, control and reflect on his own mind and emotional life, establish better relationships, get a job that had some personal meaning to him, and establish a meaningful sense of identity within a Jewish community.

Jacob wrote two versions of an essay about his use of language. Perhaps nine months after the first version and after we had done more significant therapeutic work he decided he wanted to write another essay that was clearer and better informed. He was not certain whether the second one was a replacement for the first or an elaboration. Because of this as well as the increment of self-awareness in the interval, and despite the fact that there is a significant overlap of content, I have decided to include both.

Jacob's language essay

From the first days of my life, I was in a familial environment, especially shaped by my mother, where real communication and growth never took place. This milieu was totally barren of any sense of love; instead totally defined by both mental and physical abuse. At a time before I had any sense of identity, much of the abuse was magnified by a lack of boundaries between my mother and myself. Overwhelmed with no sense of individuality, I had no help in associating words with feelings. In place of the feelings and words of a real language I was dependent upon a pseudo language spoken mainly via images grounded upon delusional beliefs.

Because this occurred so early in my life, somatic images described much of my undeveloped feelings. My pseudo language, how I expressed (or didn't express) my feelings, sheds enormous light into my lack of underlying psychological development. It took many years of therapy before I began to develop real feelings with expressive words, evolving from these largely somatic, imagistic representations, and challenging my overwhelming belief in delusions.

Over the years, Dr. Robbins provided consistent reminders about my lack of feelings and the abundance of images in their place. Only recently, eighteen years after meeting Dr. Robbins, have I become aware of how my use of images as a little boy, along with reflexively manifested rage, were carried into adult life, never developing into real feelings. Awareness provided me the opportunity to stand back and attempt to develop real feelings through understanding the images and rage, which substituted for real feelings in the past.

Though I had memories of vicious verbal and physical attacks from my mother, such as telling me that my life was not worth the pain of her episiotomy to the violent groping of her fingers in my rectum searching for "malignant" bodies, I believed that she loved me. When Doctor Robbins would disagree, I would fight with him, sometimes calling him crazy. With constant reminders, I began to realize that my rage at Dr. Robbins and the rest of the world was really rage at my mother. And that at the root, my rage was directed at myself, and then turned upon the rest of the world.

As a teenager, well before I ever met Dr. Robbins, I began having images of holding a knife in my hand and stabbing my mother. Each time that image would occur in my mind, I would have another image of being tried in a court for that murderous crime. These images haunted me. Later the violent images included people beyond my mother, and eventually forced me to leave college in my second year. What was most important was the total absence of feelings connected to these murderous images.

Early in therapy, I remember many sessions where Dr. Robbins would say, "Do you feel any anger?" or "Are you aware of any feelings"? The bottom line was that I was unable to hold any significant feelings in my mind.

This included social self-control road signs such as shame and guilt, as well as basic feelings such as caring, loving, and rage. It took repeated reminders by Dr. Robbins that I was more than bypassing these feelings. As mentioned above these feelings were not developed! For example, Dr. Robbins again and again took great pains to show that my images of shit and killing needed to be moved up to the level of feelings, like real rage. Needless to say these reminders occurred over and over again, often unheard. Now, looking back, I can see that without feelings, any hope of integration was totally impossible. The evolution of images to feelings, and then integration is a long and arduous process, still very much a part of my therapy. I can see that without the repeated support and reminders of Dr. Robbins to develop feelings, I would have been trapped in a mindless world of brittle images, antagonistic to integration.

One central delusion was that my mother really loved me, with her acts of abuse perceived by me as acts of kindness. For example, my mother believed and made me, as a helpless child, believe that I was defective, plagued by all kinds of confabulated medical maladies. She believed that defective areas of my body could be reached via my rectum, which she would penetrate with her finger. In reality she was raping me. Yet I believed this was a caring act. Brainwashed into believing that this and other abusive behavior was loving, I was totally inside-out, upside-down on any concept of caring. Thus the word "love" had a singular meaning to me. Much of the vocabulary of my pseudo language, images and words, was centered on the belief and hope that my mother really loved me.

One image which took years for me to understand and translate into words was an image of myself with a breast. Totally unaware of its meaning, it was an internal image of being merged with my mother. More than just a visual image, I always had the sense of moving my right arm down the front of my body to wipe away this extraneous growth on my body. Through long discussions with Dr. Robbins I became able to understand the meaning of this image in words. Almost never having this image any longer, it strikes me how primitive but laden with meaning this image was. Until I met Dr. Robbins I walked around totally unaware of the meaning of this image as described by words, or ultimately felt on the level of real feelings.

I want to explain how Dr. Robbins and I were able to transform the image of somatic union with my mother via her breast into something positive in my development. First Dr. Robbins understood and discussed this in a very serious way. He helped me to see intellectually that this image was a fusion of myself and my mother. In a real sense, I began learning a new language for this image. Words were used to describe and understand this image. Looking back, my feelings remained in limbo for years, while Dr. Robbins helped me gain the self-esteem to allow sufficient separation from my mother, to begin to understand the somatic rage of self-hate manifest via images of shit and shitting, self-mutilating masturbation, and violent sexual acts.

There were many images I used for rage. Prominent among them was the image of fecal matter. I had the image of myself as a brown (shitty) little Jewish boy and as shit hurled both toward others and myself. Many times I would express rage by losing control of my bowels. Having been abused so many times by my mother in my rectal area, it was no surprise that I chose this portion of my anatomy. Closely associated was my sense of impotence in the relationship with my mother. This was communicated by my memory of an image as a little boy about seven standing on a chair, soaking wet after a rain storm, with my mother removing my clothes in front of the next door neighbor. It took years of therapy with Dr. Robbins to translate this image into words, eventually developing into the constellation of real feelings: impotence, rage, shame, and fear related to being identity-less.

As a young child, I would grimace in the mirror to scare myself, as my mother scared me during the day. Young and identity-less, I unconsciously joined the world of my mother thorough such facial expressions, which along with music and images served as proxies for my undeveloped feelings. To this day I still find myself using these facial images as rageful poses. Indeed, this was part of my juvenile language of rage. It was only by reluctantly agreeing to think in therapy, that these images became translated into toxic psychological feelings related to my mother, and then after significant discussion, transformed into feelings more consistent with a reality of caring.

Not only did my mother abuse me by invading my body physically, but she also teased me sexually. I remembered and communicated these hostile acts through images as well. One image I often remembered was my mother sitting on her bed and slowly pulling up her stockings to her thighs. This image was very similar to that famous image of Mrs. Robinson in *The Graduate*. Many discussions in therapy were centered upon the result of this sexual teasing: my understanding of sexuality as an abusive activity of power, rather than a caring one of love. This confusion underpinned many of the images and words of sexuality in my pseudo language.

As mentioned earlier, my response to this abuse was prior to any development of rage as a feeling, communicated by me as this image of knifing my mother. Along with this, I also employed somatic images of sexuality in place of recognized and understood rage. In my therapy it became clear that images of women's underwear, body parts, and images much like that of Mrs. Robinson were signposts of unrecognized and undeveloped rage. My deep feelings of being subservient to my mother were portrayed by the sexual image of sucking in oral sex. This image meant "eating up," "being lost," or merging with my partner, an act of subsuming one of our identities. As mentioned earlier, sexual intercourse itself was more an image of aggression, than an affectionate act of love. Until therapy with Dr. Robbins, my sexual experience was driven as an attack at myself and others, my sadistic rage at myself and my mother.

Impotence and rage were central feelings of my childhood. Needless to say they continue to haunt me in my adulthood. When I feel impotent and my rage is high, I am at a real loss for words, a real sense of aphasia. I'm sure this represents a regression to a state when I had no vocabulary, totally unable to relate as an individual to the world around myself. A healthy connection of feelings and words would have been fostered by a loving mother. In my case, my mother did everything within her power to retard that development. It took years of persistent therapy with Dr. Robbins for me to recognize and translate these images into an identity of real feelings, like rage, caring, impotence. It has been a long trip from my childhood concrete, sadistic images such as excrement and violent sexual experience, to my understanding of rage as a real feeling; and most important, the recognition and integration of love and caring as the central motivating feelings of my life.

My pseudo language provided a window into what would become the foundation and development of my feelings. My language was primitive with few words, but images, grounded on delusional beliefs. Years of therapy with Dr. Robbins challenged these deeply distorted beliefs, and through thinking began a process of finding words to describe these persistent images. Thinking about these images began to provide a vocabulary, one that could begin to describe my deep-seated beliefs and resulting imagery. Without the words of real language there could be no thinking, no rational challenge to my delusional beliefs, and no development and integration of real feelings.

Jacob's second essay titled "Pseudo Language"

The purpose of this essay is to illustrate my journey from pseudo language to real language. My therapy with Dr. Robbins began seventeen years ago. Looking back, I can see how disconnected I was. By this I mean, not only an alienation from my self, but a lack of belonging to the outside world. I do remember sitting across from Dr. Robbins keeping warm with a very heavy coat. I had not the words to describe my tragic aloneness, only the somatic feeling of coldness.

This world began for me with a mother whose sole connection to me was destructive, both physically as well as psychologically. Comments like, "You weren't worth the pain of my episiotomy," to the physical invasion of my body through her finger in my rectum, made this connection, one of disconnection. There was no one to trust, no one to provide the basis of any love for myself or the world. Looking back, it was a world of connected disconnectedness.

For me as a little boy there was no language to express this inexpressible condition. If I had my own self, my own identity, I would have had the thoughts and a language to express this situation. I would have begun constructing the feelings of pain and sorrow, commensurate with such treatment. But I was all alone, no mind to fathom this terrible situation. In therapy, the central image that I used over and over to describe this horrible situation was the feeling of a breast on my right upper body. My response to this unwanted lump on my upper torso was thoughtless and reflexively somatic: a feeling of pushing this breast off my body, by sweeping my forearm down.

From the very first meetings with Dr. Robbins, I described my world in a series of somatic images. My dark feeling of doom was described by the fear that I was going to die from some deadly disease. This sense of impending death was one of my mother's most favorite dramas. Many times Dr. Robbins would ask, "What feelings do you have?" And my response was always empty, because I really had no feelings. What I understood as love was not the real feeling of love, but some abstract definition that had no support in the real world. In this abstract definition my mother "loved" me, even though she was actively engaged in my destruction. I had developed no feelings of love for myself, only the belief that I was a defective, described by the image of a "little brown Jewish boy."

I'd like to say that it was the two of us, myself and Dr. Robbins, who created the goal of translating these images into real feelings. For most of my therapy, it was only Dr. Robbins, while I continued to act out the feelings with expression of primitive images. Finally, in this last year I have joined him and we have begun to work together. The question has always been the same, "What am I really feeling; translate the images into real feelings; hold the feelings inside myself as a separate person." In short, describe myself as I really am, with a language consistent with my real feelings.

Something of which I have become increasingly aware is that my feelings were not buried, only to be later discovered; in fact they were not there. Primary among these undeveloped feelings were my vulnerability, impotence, and rage. Certainly there were images which described these at most inchoate feelings, such as when my mother undressed me at the age of six, soaking wet from a rain storm, in front of our next door neighbor. Or when my mother had no second thought of pushing her finger into my rectum in search of some hidden demon of somatic defectiveness. Or my own image of escaping the world and destroying myself, when I ran in front if a car and was hit, resulting in a fractured skull and concussion. And finally my image of a knife, with which I fantasized I would kill my mother, and over and over used to express my hostility to Dr. Robbins. These images were the fractured pieces of a pseudo language, a "language" before the development of a language, before the development of feelings to support a language.

As mentioned earlier, these images were all that represented the expression of my feelings. Primary among them were those of sexual imagery. Along with my mother assaulting me somatically and psychologically, she teased me sexually as a young child. Thus sex and the potency of my penis became an image of power, violently attacking myself through masturbation, as well as assaulting sexual partners. In short my penis became a sword of destruction. My life was filled with images of destruction, both to myself and the outside world. I really could not understand the comments that Dr. Robbins made concerning the violence of my sexual "feelings." I thought I was a real nice guy with ordinary desires. In fact, sex was not an expression of love, it was an image of violence.

An important hindrance to my understanding the depth of my involvement with images as a pseudo language, was my investment in grandiosity. This allowed me to escape my emptiness and anger directed at myself and others including destruction of my ability to be a professional mathematician, my rage at women, my undifferentiated anger at the world and the destruction of my family leading to eventual divorce. Moving away from this grandiosity, seeing myself as I really am, has taken many hours of work: understanding Dr. Robbins and myself as separate people in a relationship designed to understand the truth of the past, and how it affects my thinking. In short, I finally have the chance to understand my pain, love myself and understand others. I am finally seeing Dr. Robbins as a caring person, who has been helping me to be caring.

In a real sense, I am involved with Dr. Robbins in understanding my past with grief, the sadness of knowing I was not loved. It has been hard for me to drop my belief that I am a defective person. I have hung onto that belief with the image of me as a "little brown Jewish boy." Dr. Robbins and I have spent much time in understanding this image: a vulnerable (Jewish) little boy who is brown (shit). Moving from this belief to a caring consideration of who I really am is ongoing work. Seeing the real feelings I have, like the fear of being alone (on my own), owning up to my guilt, understanding and holding the pain of my behavior in the past, taking responsibility for myself as a separate person is constant work (many times at Dr. Robbins's urging). The outcome for me is becoming a more caring and loving person, who can build a real language, based on the truth of my feelings.

Through the ongoing help and direction of Dr. Robbins, I have tried to turn away from my own deception of grandiosity to working on understanding my imagistic thinking and developing real feelings. The image of the breast fused to my body has come to mean that I am merging identities with my mother, with all of the feelings of impotence and rage. Knowing this has provided me internal direction, as I attempt to develop a separate, real identity. A good example is understanding my image of being "a little brown Jewish boy." With the ongoing help of Dr. Robbins, I was able to join a Jewish temple, understand being Jewish as an image of vulnerability associated with making myself the target of my rage, and develop a positive feeling of self-esteem. In the big picture, moving past this imagistic belief has allowed me to step back and understand my feelings of impotence toward my mother and rage at myself and others. I have also tried to be aware of the imagistic meaning of my penis as a weapon. Understanding this as an object employed in fulfillment of rage, I have been able to understand my rage and integrate sexuality as an instrument of love.

In conclusion, my conversion from the language of images to one based on feelings has provided me the real option of being loving. All of the images I have employed, the fused breast, the little brown Jewish boy, and my penis as a sword, have been shallow one dimensional views of myself. With the help of Dr. Robbins, understanding these images has provided me the opportunity to develop real feelings. As a little child, in my relationship with my mother, love was totally absent. Without the foundation of love, images had been my only mode of communication. In fact holding feelings as a separate person has been very difficult for me. But now I have the real alternative of experiencing feelings like pain, joy, guilt, and love. My work in therapy has been to take these feelings and manufacture an individual, separate, and caring self. This identity is understood by me and communicated to the outside world through a language based on real feelings.

Discussion

Instead of using words to describe basic emotions and associated thoughts, and by so doing consolidate a cohesive sense of self as a basis for realistic adaptive actions, Jacob experienced an undifferentiated amalgam of evanescent snapshot-like images of important incidents from childhood or depictions of current impulses; somatic sensations of emptiness, coldness, bowel and penile sensations and related preoccupations with parts of his body and their function, and associated motor behavior. He was impelled to act on hostile impulses the nature of which he was unaware, and make associated attempts to control and destroy the autonomy of the other, because in his undifferentiated and unintegrated psyche he mis-perceived the hostility as emanating from the other and had to defend himself against the belief the other was trying to destroy his identity. He had no sense of having emotions of his own, but perceived himself and the world in an undifferentiated way that I came to label kill or be killed. Language – his words and those of others – was a tool of action, force and manipulation. It conveyed the belief he was being invaded and his identity was being taken over ("sucking up"), and reciprocally he was constantly looking for problems and badness in the other that had to be exterminated. Words and concepts were mislabeled; as Jacob writes, "acts of rage perceived as acts of kindness."

Although he reported to me countless vivid detailed images of mother assaulting, controlling and rejecting him physically and verbally in childhood, they were not stable mental representations linked with appropriate emotions. As she had told him these were loving acts he maintained the conviction they had a loving relationship and believed I was crazy when I suggested they told another story. He relentlessly attacked me in a parody of psychoanalytic interpretation. He could not articulate emotions but regularly had images of having a knife when we talked, of me "sitting in shit," of probing my anus as his mother had done to him, of assaulting one of my children, and many more, without awareness in representational reflective emotional thought of what he was "saying."

Even when he had recourse to tapes of our sessions he regularly used them not in the language of reflective thought, but as evidence within which to find faults and defects in me in what I had said, attributing in an undifferentiated way to my words, as he often inaccurately recalled them, his own unintegrated lethally hostile intentions. His unconscious objective was to obliterate any sense of personal separateness and to actualize a world in which the other was eliminated as the unrecognized solution to avoiding what was intolerable in himself. His goal was to be able to talk his unexamined language of hatred and omnipotent grandiosity unimpeded by any response from me that would require him to control and reflect on what he was saying. At the same time, as must have been the case with his mother during the earliest attachment phase, he required my presence as a concrete entity or screen on which to perceive the unrepresented parts of himself. He had no awareness of his diffuse rage and its undifferentiated direction toward himself and others. Needless to say, because Jacob lived in a world where self-regulation and control and the work necessary for these things were unknown, he had not developed language for appropriate social control emotions such as shame and guilt.

In lieu of a language-based sense of self Jacob developed a delusional system based on the extreme and concrete belief he was diseased excrement, a "brown Jewish boy" who was fatally physically defective. He attached this to one physical aspect or another and regularly and literally interpreted this to mean he was about to die, requiring constant medical ministrations in thoughtless reenactment of what his mother had done to him and told him. It was all so real we were unable to talk about his lack of self-worth and his self-hatred as an idea he had learned. His somatized belief in his utter worthlessness was associated with any hint or bit of feedback that he might have a problem, so that in his undifferentiated way it led him to interpret any attempt I made to help him see himself as an attack on his being, stimulating him to launch the most vicious "interpretive" assaults on me.

In apparent compensation he erected a false self, based on a sense of know-it-all grandiosity and omnipotence, involving fabrication of his life story and accomplishments, and a know-it-all attitude that involved constant fault-finding and giving advice to others. He used this to rationalize his belief he did not need anyone else in his life even as he was clearly unable to live independently and required a masochistic person in the form of unsuspecting therapist or woman whom he could attack both verbally and with poorly concealed sexual sadism while expecting from that person total agreement, love and admiration. In his belief system he was acting caring when in fact he treated people, especially women, much the way his mother had treated him. He could not tolerate feedback and interpreted it as attack. Of necessity I gave him more of that than he had ever gotten. In return he attacked me in a manner of which he was totally unaware, called me crazy, and for a time in actual imagery perceived me as a monster. As he gradually and painfully became more self-aware he repeatedly reported a feeling of impotent aphasia inconsistent with his large formal vocabulary, as he realized he literally had no language with which to accurately describe his emotional self and his emotions.

Jacob's undifferentiated primordial consciousness and its language which confused love and hate and misattributed his mental state to me and others, was based on his abysmal lack of a sense of self-worth, which for him was a concrete physical reality and not an idea, and on his inability to care about himself and hence anyone else.

Chapter 18

Our languages and our selves
Discussion and conclusion

In the preceding pages I have considered language, defined to encompass pre-speech comprehension as well as verbal expression, as the essential vehicle, both private and social, of one's sense of self. It expresses *who we think* (or more accurately who we believe) we are and not necessarily an "objective" or realistic assessment. I have described the fundamentally bilingual nature of human beings based on two qualitatively different forms of consciousness and the language expression unique to each. What we commonly think of when we refer to language, the expression of reflective representational thought, is actually a "second language." We begin life in a state we share with other animals, primordial consciousness, initially expressed in psychologically undifferentiated interactions with the primary caregiver in the mother tongue, that some call motherese. While the mother tongue provides the socialization that facilitates development of the second language, it is not a stage in development that is lost or transformed in the course of development, like the umbilical cord or baby teeth, but a qualitatively distinctive manifestation of mind that uses language in a unique manner and that persists throughout life in a variety of manifestations, some simply different or unusual, others seemingly normal in their context, and still others that we label abnormal.

The language of primordial consciousness is somatic, concrete, performative or instrumental. It is a language of "it is" or "I am" not "I think it is" or "I think, therefore I am." It is the experience of being, a sense of agency expressed in enactments, using gestures, body expressions, vocalizations and actions. It is a language of pressure and compliance, taking in, withholding and expelling. Primordial consciousness articulates evanescent affect-laden images but does not contain, represent and associate them as ideas and memories associated with emotions that give them meaning. Its narrative thread is organized by affect tones, sensory-perceptual experiences and somatic sensations, not by association of ideas related by emotion or by sequences dependent upon time, memory, or reflective logic. It is a language of here and now without clear distinction between past and present. The past is always being recreated and reenacted.

The language of primordial consciousness is solipsistic. It is the language of a person unable to become a psychologically separate individual and function within a world of separate persons and a reality that may differ from the content of one's mind. While the capacity to make formal distinctions is intact, from a psychological perspective it is undifferentiated with regard to external and internal reality, between self and other. This is in contrast to the language of reflective representational thought which recognizes a world of separate selves and an objective reality distinctive from the self. The person treats the contents of his or her own mind as though they are present in or emanating from the external world. This is why it is such a powerful language of belief or certainty, and why persons with similar beliefs bond together so readily and powerfully, whether it be parents and infants, people attending a rock concert or a religious revival, political extremists or cult members. In situations where the expression of primordial consciousness is not contextually shared with others who are functioning in reflective representational consciousness that differentiates internal from external reality, there is a major collision of realities. The latter group may look upon the ideation of the former as myth or fantasy, for instance when commenting on members of a tribal culture or a religious group, or a culture of antiquity like the ancient Greeks; or as delusional or magical thinking, in the instance of psychosis. The former group believes the latter just does not know what is right and true. When the mentation of primordial consciousness is shared it represents a view of the world that expresses itself in the form of social movements or the social fabric of entire tribes or nations.

As both reflective representational thought and primordial consciousness ultimately come to share the same formal language structure, vocabulary, and fund of knowledge, the fact that language is being used to express an undifferentiated state of belief and enactment may not be apparent to the observer whose modus operandi and expectation is that language is equivalent to representational symbolic thought, except in egregious instances such as severe psychosis. One of the numerous distinctions, that I refer to throughout the book, is that first person pronouns denote agency and being but not reflection, and second and third person pronouns do not have the "I-thou" meaning they do in reflective representational thought. The "you" and the "we" of powerful oratory have this quality of concreteness and attribution and in conjunction with the powerful "I" that indicates being and agency but no reflection exerts powerful performative coercive force on the mind of the listener.

The dual nature of language sheds light on the current controversy within linguistics about the origin and defining characteristics of language. The belief that there is but one hardwired language template whose phenomenological hallmark is recursion is based on the implicit myopic assumption that all language is the expression of reflective representational thought. However, the belief of some who claim that if there are languages that lack recursion that proves language is the learned product of its particular social context is also incorrect. Recognition of the existence of two conscious mental processes each with its own language establishes the legitimacy of language without recursion and leaves the question of the relative contributions of nature and nurture a subject of further investigation.

The concept of two qualitatively different uses of language illuminates another controversy, between those who believe language and thought are isomorphic and those who believe they are different expressions of mind and self. This controversy is based on a similar unidimensionally myopic fallacy, but in this instance one that is opposite; one that equates thought with a process like primordial consciousness, that cannot be encompassed by a language presumed to have the characteristics we associate with reflective representational mind. The evidence that language may be "of two minds" supports the conclusion that language can express thought – of two different kinds.

The two languages with which we frame our mental activity comprise primarily if not exclusively our fundamental sense of self in relation to the world. Primordial consciousness is our first language, the mother tongue, the language of solipsism or global unity, derived from the mother-infant interactions that commence *in utero*. Learning primordial consciousness and its language is a process that occurs between the last trimester of gestation, once the brain matures sufficiently to support REM and auditory activity, and approximately 5 years of age, but is for the most part completed by the end of the first half year or so of life. At some point during the second year, if a secure and accurate foundation of self has been created during the initial undifferentiated phase of mothering, the infant commences the process of separation from primary caregivers and recognition of the separateness of self and others, and the learning of a second language that expresses it, the language of reflective representational thought. This learning process spans many years as the brain slowly matures, and it enables the person to concretely separate from the primary family and establish a secure sense of self in relation to a world of separate others. Primordial consciousness and the capacity to express it under suitable circumstances persists in adult life. Under ordinary circumstances its use is increasingly regulated by reflective representational thought in ways that are realistic and adaptive.

The language of primordial consciousness can be used in many situations, for many purposes. Some of these are looked upon as "normal," and others "abnormal." The use of quotation marks is intended to highlight that normality and pathology are social judgments. There are many "normal" uses of primordial consciousness in everyday life.

The examples of aberration in adult language I have presented each involve use of the language of primordial consciousness in contextually socially inappropriate settings to express distorted understandings of self and world. The person using the language and sometimes the person or persons toward whom it is directed as well, believe that the utterances and the communication are in the language of reflective representational thought. There may be no awareness that the pair are "speaking different languages," one assuming an undifferentiated or fused sense of the world and the other supporting a view of separate persons and separation of intrapsychic and external realities. In such instances the two are unwittingly communicating at cross-purposes. Language aberrations are not easily categorized as normal or abnormal. Some may be associated with behavior that is labeled as abnormal, some may relate to uses of primordial consciousness that cause the subject distress and lead to seeking therapeutic help, while others go unnoticed as they do not disrupt the interpersonal/social context in which they occur in any obvious way.

There are three components to language aberration: the presence of primordial consciousness and its language in situations where it is contextually inappropriate and maladaptive; its use to express distorted content about self and world; and its use to maintain a fused or undifferentiated relationship with the primary caregiver from whom the subject has not had the support and security necessary to become a separate self-valuing self-sustaining individual. This last fact can only be uncovered in the transference relationship of intensive analytic therapy as it is enacted in the present rather than remembered as a past event. In place of a sufficiently secure attachment based on caring, which is the basis for development of a separate individuated self, there remains a solipsistic state of identity or fusion (not identification) with the destructive characteristics of the mothering person. In such instances language does not reflect the core physical emotional self but a destructive entanglement with the other, both internalized and external.

Without a primary caring, realistically mirroring and guiding interaction language can neither begin to express one's separate unique self nor serve as a symbolic medium of exchange of meanings with other separate selves. When the necessary attachment and social facilitation is missing the language of primordial consciousness persists into adult life in situations in which it is no longer appropriate and adaptive because it is a language that does not support separation from the primary caregiver. In such instances its content reflects the disturbed, unrealistic and maladaptive beliefs about self and world that have interfered with development of a mature separate life. Because the bilingual nature of mind and its respective languages, and the relationship of primordial consciousness to the initial identity with mother, have been inadequately appreciated, the extent to which the formal language of separateness masks a fundamental failure of separation and individuation in many people has been inadequately appreciated.

It is important to reiterate that the formal sensory-perceptual apparatus of the person using language in an aberrant fashion, and the instrumental actions that come from it and are necessary for adaptive basic living, are intact, and indeed, as illustrated by examples like Lisabeth's may be exceptional. For instance, a person like Jacob who is unable to contain and represent his rage and differentiate it from others can drive a car accurately, even with exceptional skill, while cutting off other drivers and giving them "the finger" based on the belief that in his world of undifferentiated rage they are out to get him. It is the meanings of the perceptions and actions that direct or are associated with the cognition that are distorted.

Who we think we are, who others think we are, and who we think others are, the relationship of self and world, can be very confusing. My purpose has been to articulate the reasons for and manifestations of this confusion. People who speak the same language often speak "foreign" languages if considered from a deeper psychological perspective. A fundamental language-based psychological disorientation as to whether two persons are in an undifferentiated one person world or a separate two (or more) person world pervades many social interactions unbeknown to the participants. From this perspective the answer to the question, "Who do you think you are?" might reside in the answer to a deeper question: "Do you know what language or languages you and the other are speaking?"

References

Ainsworth, M. D. S. (1982). Attachment: Retrospect and prospect. In: C. Parkes, & J. Stevenson-Hinde (Eds.), *The Place of Attachment in Human Behavior*. New York: Basic Books, pp. 3–30.

Ainsworth, M. D. S., Blehar, M. C., Waters, E., & Wall, S. (1978). *Patterns of Attachment: A Psychological Study of the Strange Situation*. Hillsdale, NJ: Erlbaum.

Allport, G. W. (1937). *Personality: A Psychological Interpretation*. New York: Holt.

Best, C., & McRoberts, G. (2003). Infant perception of non-native consonant contrasts that adults assimilate in different ways. *Language and Speech*, 46: 183–216.

Bettes, B. (1988). Maternal depression and motherese: Temporal and intonational features. *Child Development*, 59: 1089–1096.

Blair, G. (2000). *The Trumps: Three Generations That Built an Empire*. New York: Simon & Schuster.

Boston Change Process Study Group (BCPSG) (2007). The foundational level of psychodynamic meaning: Implicit process in relation to conflict, defense and the dynamic unconscious. *International Journal of Psychoanalysis*, 88: 843–860.

Bowlby, J. (1969). *Attachment and Loss, Vol. I: Attachment*. London: Hogarth Press and the Institute of Psycho-Analysis.

Britton, R. (1998). *Belief and Imagination*. London: Routledge.

Bucci, W. (1997). Discourse patterns in "good" and troubled hours: A multiple code interpretation. *Journal of the American Psychoanalytic Association*, 45: 155–187.

Bucci, W. (2000). Pathways of emotional communication. *Psychoanalytic Inquiry*, 21: 40–70.

Bucci, W. (2011). The interplay of subsymbolic and symbolic processes in psychoanalytic treatment: It takes two to tango—But who knows the steps, who's the leader? The choreography of the psychoanalytic interchange. *Psychoanalytic Dialogues*, 21: 45–54.

Burnham, D., Kitamura, C., & Vollmer-Conna, U. (2002). What's new, pussycat? On talking to babies and animals. *Science*, 296: 1435.

Burns, R. (1786). *Complete Poems and Songs of Robert Burns*. London: Waverley Books, 2012.

Capellini, I., Preston, B., McNamara, P., Barton, R., & Nunn, C. (2009). Ecological constraints on mammalian sleep architecture. In: P. McNamara, R. Barton, & L. Nunn (Eds.), *Phylogeny of Sleep*. Cambridge: Cambridge University Press.

Choi, J., Cutler, A., & Broersma, M. (2017). Early development of abstract language knowledge: Evidence from perception-production transfer of birth-language memory. *Royal Society Open Science*, 4: 160–166.
Chomsky, N. (1965). *Aspects of the Theory of Syntax*. Cambridge, MA: MIT Press.
Chomsky, N. (1978). *Syntactic Structures*. Berlin: Mouton.
Church, J. (1966). *Language and the Discovery of Reality*. New York: Vintage Books.
Condon, W., & Sander, L. (1974). Neonate movement is synchronized with adult speech: Interactional participation and language acquisition. *Science*, 183: 99–101.
Damasio, A. (1999). *The Feeling of What Happens: Body and Emotion in the Making of Consciousness*. New York: Harcourt Brace.
Darwin, C. (1871). *The Descent of Man, and Selection in Relation to Sex*. London: Forgotten Books, 2015.
Dennett, D. (1986). Julian Jaynes's Software Archeology. *Canadian Psychology*, 27: 149–154.
D'Odorico, L., & Jacob, V. (2006). Prosodic and lexical aspects of maternal linguistic input to late-talking toddlers. *International Journal of Language and Communication Disorders*, 41: 293–311.
Durkin, K., Rutter, D., & Tucker, H. (1982). Social interaction and language acquisition: Motherese help you. *First Language*, 3: 107–120.
Dylan, B. (1963). *Eleven Outlined Epitaphs*. Cologne, Germany: Kiepenheuer & Witsch.
Eliade, M. (1964). *Shamanism: Archaic Techniques of Ecstasy*. New York: Pantheon Books.
Emde, R. (1993). Epilogue: A beginning – Research approaches and expanding horizons for psychoanalysis. *Journal of the American Psychoanalytic Association*, 41S: 411–424.
Erreich, A. (2003). A modest proposal: (Re)defining unconscious fantasy. *Psychoanalytic Quarterly*, 72: 541–574.
Everett, D. (2005). Cultural constraints on grammar and cognition in Piraha: Another look at the design features of human language. *Current Anthropology*, 46: 621–646.
Everett, D. (2008). *Don't Sleep, There Are Snakes: Life and Language in the Amazon Jungle*. New York: Pantheon Books.
Fabrega, H., & Silver, S. (1970). Some social and psychological properties of Zinacanteco Shamans. *Behavioral Science*, 15: 471–486.
Ferguson, C. (1964). Baby talk in six languages. *American Anthropologist*, 66: 103–114.
Fernald, A. (1993). Approval and disapproval: Infant responsiveness to vocal affect in familiar and unfamiliar languages. *Child Development*, 64: 657–674.
Fernald, A. (1996). The onset of language development. In: P. Bloom (Ed), *Language Acquisition: Core Readings*. Cambridge, MA: MIT Press, pp. 51–94.
Fernald, A., & Kuhl, P. (1987). Acoustic determinants of infant preference for motherese speech. *Infant Behavior & Development*, 10: 279–293.
Fernald, A., & Simon, T. (1984). Expanded intonation contours in mothers' speech to newborns. *Developmental Psychology*, 20: 104–113.
Fleck, L. (1935). *Genesis and Development of a Scientific Fact*. Chicago: University of Chicago Press, 1981.

Fleck, L. (1947). To look, to see, to know. *Boston Studies in the Philosophy of Science*, New York: Springer, 81: 129–151.

Fonagy, P., & Target, M. (1997). Attachment and reflective function: Their role in self organization. *Development and Psychopathology*, 9: 679–700.

Fraiberg, S. (1959). *The Magic Years: Understanding and Handling the Problems of Early Childhood.* New York: Charles Scribner's Sons.

Freud, S. (1900a). *The Interpretation of Dreams. S. E.*, 4–5. London: Hogarth Press.

Freud, S. (1905d). *Three Essays on the Theory of Sexuality. S. E.*, 5. London: Hogarth Press.

Freud, S. (1911b). Formulations on the two principles of mental functioning. *S. E.*, 12. London: Hogarth Press.

Freud, S. (1915e). The unconscious. *S. E.*, 14: 166–215. London: Hogarth Press.

Freud, S. (1940e). Splitting of the ego in the process of defence. *S. E.*, 23. London: Hogarth Press.

Galatzer-Levy, R., & Cohler, B. (1993). *The Essential Other: A Developmental Psychology of the Self.* New York: Basic Books.

Gazzaniga, M. (1967). The split brain in man. *Scientific American*, 217: 24–29.

Glucksberg, S., & Danks, J. (1975). *Experimental Psycholinguistics: An Introduction.* Hillsdale, NJ: Erlbaum.

Gottlieb, A. (2004). *The Afterlife Is Where We Come From: The Culture of Infancy in West Africa.* Chicago: University of Chicago Press.

Greenspan, S., & Shanker, S. (2005). *The First Idea: How Symbols, Language and Intelligence Evolved from Our Primate Ancestors to Modern Humans.* Cambridge, MA: Da Capo Press.

Grieser, D., & Kuhl, P. (1988). Maternal speech to infants in a tonal language: Support for universal prosodic features in motherese. *Developmental Psychology*, 24: 14–20.

Halber, D. (2017). 10 ways that animals are smarter than you think. *Boston Globe*, January 25.

Hauser, M., Chomsky, N., & Fitch, W. (2002). The faculty of language: What is it, who has it, and how did it evolve? *Science*, 298: 1569–1579.

Herrera, E., Reissland, N., & Shepherd, J. (2004). Maternal touch and maternal child-directed speech: Effects of depressed mood in the postnatal period. *Journal of Affective Disorders*, 81: 29–39.

Hesse, E., & Main, M. (2000). Disorganized infant, child, and adult attachment. *Journal of the American Psychoanalytic Association*, 48: 1097–1127.

Imada, T., Zhang, Y., Cheour, M., Taulu, S., Ahonen, A., & Kuhl, P. (2006). Infant speech perception activates Broca's area: A developmental magnetoencephalography study. *Neuroreport*, 17: 957–962.

Isaacs, S. (1948). The nature and function of phantasy. *International Journal of Psychoanalysis*, 29: 73–97.

Jacques, F. (1991). *Difference and Subjectivity: Dialogue and Personal Identity.* New Haven, CT: Yale University Press.

Jaynes, J. (1976). *The Origin of Consciousness in the Breakdown of the Bicameral Mind.* New York: Houghton Mifflin.

Johnson, J., & Newport, E. (1989). Critical period effects in second language learning: The influence of maturation state on the acquisition of English as a second language. *Cognitive Psychology*, 21: 60–99.

Jones, E. (1918). The theory of symbolism. *British Journal of Psychology*, 9: 181–229.
Jung, C. G. (1912). Two kinds of thinking. In: *Symbols of Transformation*. Bollingen Series XX Vol. 5. F.R.C. Hull (Trans.). *The Basic Writings of C. G. Jung*. V. De Laszlo (Ed.), New York: The Modern Library (1959), pp. 10–36.
Kanai, R., Feilden, T., Firth, C., & Rees, G. (2011). Political orientations are correlated with brain structure in young adults. *Current Biology*, 21: 677–680.
Klein, M. (1930). The importance of symbol-formation in the development of the ego. In: *Love, Guilt and Reparation and Other Works 1921–1945*. London: Hogarth Press, 1975, pp. 219–232.
Klein, M. (1946). Notes on some schizoid mechanisms. In: *Envy and Gratitude and Other Works, 1946–1963*. London: Hogarth Press, pp. 1–24.
Kolata, G. (1984). Studying learning in the womb. *Science*, 225: 302–303.
Kracke, W. (1999). A language of dreaming: Dreams of an Amazonian insomniac. *International Journal of Psychoanalysis*, 80: 257–271.
Kuhl, P. (2010). Brain mechanisms in early language acquisition. *Neuron*, 67: 713–727.
Kuhl, P., & Meltzoff, A. (1996). Infant vocalizations in response to speech: Vocal imitation and developmental change. *Journal of the Acoustic Society of America*, 100: 2425–2438.
Lenneberg, E. (1967). *Biological Foundations of Language*. New York: John Wiley & Sons.
Litowitz, B. (2009). Explorations in subjectivity, agency, and responsibility. *Annual of Psychoanalysis*, 36/37: 230–245.
Litowitz, B. (2011). From dyad to dialogue: Language and the early relationship in American psychoanalytic theory. *Journal of the American Psychoanalytic Association*, 59(3): 483–507.
Locke, J. (1714). *An Essay Concerning Human Understanding*. Chapter X, Book III. In: *The Complete Works of John Locke*. London: Delphi Classics, 2017, p. 230.
Lyons-Ruth, K. (1999). The two-person unconscious: Intersubjective dialogue, enactive relational representation, and the emergence of new forms of relational organization. *Psychoanalytic Inquiry*, 19: 576–617.
Lyons-Ruth, K. (2003). Dissociation and the parent-infant dialogue. *Journal of the American Psychoanalytic Association*, 51: 883–911.
Mahler, M., Pine, F., & Bergman, A. (1975). *The Psychological Birth of the Human Infant*. New York: Basic Books.
Masataka, N. (1998). Perception of motherese in Japanese sign language by 6-month-old hearing infants. *Developmental Psychology*, 34: 241–246.
Matte-Blanco, I. (1975). *The Unconscious as Infinite Sets: An Essay in Bi–logic*. London: Duckworth.
Matte-Blanco, I. (1988). *Thinking, Feeling, and Being: Clinical Reflections on the Fundamental Antinomy of Human Beings and World*. London: New Library of Psycho-Analysis.
McNeill, D. (1970). *The Acquisition of Language: The Study of Developmental Psycholinguistics*. New York: Harper & Row.
Mehler, J., & Christophe, A. (2000). Acquisition of languages: Infant and adult data. In: M. Gazzaniga (Ed.), *The New Cognitive Neurosciences*. Cambridge, MA and London: MIT Press.

Meissner, W. (2008). The role of language in the development of the self. I: Language acquisition. *Psychoanalytic Psychology*, 25: 26–46.

Meltzoff, A., & Decety, J. (2003). What imitation tells us about social cognition: A rapprochement between developmental psychology and cognitive neuroscience. *Philosophical Transactions of the Royal Society of London. Biological Science*, 358: 491–500.

Moffic, H. S. (1987). What about the bicameral mind? *American Journal of Psychiatry*, 144: 696.

Moon, C., Randall, D., Zernzach, R., & Kuhl, P. (2015). Mothers say "baby" and their newborns do not choose to listen: A behavioral preference study to compare with ERP results. *Frontiers in Human Neuroscience*, 9: 153.

Nakashima-Degarrod, L. (1989). *Dream Interpretation among the Mapuche Indians of Chile*. Ann Arbor, MI: University of Michigan Dissertation Information Service.

Nicholson, S. (Ed.) (1987). *Shamanism*. Wheaton, IL: The Theosophical Publishing House.

Partanen, E., Kujala, T., Naatanin, R., Liitola, A., Sambeth, A., & Huotilainen, N. (2013). Learning-induced neural plasticity of speech before birth. *Proceedings of the American Academy of Sciences*, 110: 15145–15150.

Paus, T., Zijdembos, A., Worsele, K., Collins, L., Blumenthal, J., Geidd, J., Rapoport, J., Evans A., et al. (1999). Structural maturation of neural pathways in children and adolescents: In vivo study. *Science*, 283: 1908–1911.

Piaget, J. (1936). *The Origins of Intelligence in Children*. New York: International Universities Press, 1952.

Pinker, S. (1994). *The Language Instinct: How the Mind Creates Language*. New York: William Morrow & Co.

Popper, K., & Eccles, J. (1985). *The Self and Its Brain*. New York: Springer.

Prechtel, M. (2012). *The Unlikely Peace at Cuchumaquic*. Berkeley, CA: North Atlantic Books.

Pulvermuller, F. (2005). Brain mechanisms linking language to action. *National Review of Neuroscience*; 6: 574–582.

Rivera-Gaxiola, M., Silvia-Pereyra, J., & Kuhl, P. (2005). Brain potentials to native and non-native speech: Contrasts in 7- and 11-month-old American infants. *Developmental Science*, 8: 162–172.

Rizzolatti, G. (2005).The mirror neuron system and imitation. In: S. Hurley, & N. Chater, (Eds.), *Perspectives on Imitation: From Neuroscience to Social Science – I: Mechanisms of Imitation and Imitation in Animals*. Cambridge, MA: MIT Press, pp. 55–76.

Rizzolatti, G., & Craighero, L. (2004). The mirror-neuron system. *Annual Review of Neuroscience*; 27: 169–192.

Rizzuto, A.-M. (1988). Transference, language, and affect in the treatment of bulimarexia. *International Journal of Psychoanalysis*, 69: 369–387.

Rizzuto, A.-M. (2002). Speech events, language development and the clinical situation. *International Journal of Psychoanalysis*, 83: 1325–1343.

Rizzuto, A.-M. (2003). Psychoanalysis: The transformation of the subject by the spoken word. *Psychoanalytic Quarterly*, 72: 287–323.

Robbins, M. (1969). On the psychology of artistic creativity. *Psychoanalytic Study of the Child*, 24: 227–251.

Robbins, M. (1993). *Experiences of Schizophrenia: An Integration of the Personal, Scientific and Therapeutic*. New York: Guilford Press.
Robbins, M. (1996). *Conceiving of Personality*. New Haven, CT: Yale University Press.
Robbins, M. (2002). The language of schizophrenia and the world of delusion. *International Journal of Psychoanalysis*, 83: 383–405.
Robbins, M. (2004). Another look at dreaming: Disentangling Freud's primary and secondary process theories. *Journal of the American Psychoanalytic Association*, 52: 355–384.
Robbins, M. (2008). Primary mental expression: Freud, Klein and beyond. *Journal of the American Psychoanalytic Association*, 56: 177–202.
Robbins, M. (2011). *The Primordial Mind in Health and Illness: A Cross–Cultural Perspective*. London & New York: Routledge.
Robbins, M. (2015). The "royal road" – to what? *Annual of Psychoanalysis*, 38: 196–214.
Robbins, M. (2018). *The primary process: Freud's profound yet neglected contribution to the psychology of consciousness*. Psychoanalytic Inquiry, 38.
Robertson, J., & Robertson, J. (1971). Young children in brief separation – A fresh look. *Psychoanalytic Study of the Child*, 26: 264–315.
Rommetveit, R. (1974). *On Message Structure: A Framework for the Study of Language and Communication*. New York: Wiley.
Scherer, M. (2017). Interview with Donald Trump as summarized by New York Times Editorial Board. *New York Times*, March 23.
Schwab, K., Groh, T., Schwab, M., & Witte, H. (2009). Nonlinear analysis and modeling of cortical activation and deactivation patterns in the immature fetal electrocorticogram. *Chaos. An Interdisciplinary Journal of Nonlinear Science*, 19. Retrieved from https://www.ncbi.nlm.nih.gov/pubmed/19335015.
Segal, H. (1957). Notes on symbol formation. *International Journal of Psychoanalysis*, 38: 39–45.
Segal, H. (1978). On symbolism. *International Journal of Psychoanalysis*, 59: 315–319.
Segal, H. (1994). Phantasy and reality. *International Journal of Psychoanalysis*, 75: 395–401.
Shear, M. D. (2017). What Trump's Time interview shows about his thinking. *New York Times*, March 23.
Sharpless, E. (1985). Identity formation as reflected in the acquisition of personal pronouns. *Journal of the American Psychoanalytic Association*, 71: 861–885.
Shelton, R. (1987). *No Direction Home: The Life and Music of Bob Dylan*. London: Penguin Books.
Sperry, R. W. (1961). Cerebral organization and behavior: The split brain behaves in many respects like two separate brains, providing new research possibilities. *Science*, 133: 1749–1757.
Spitz, R. (1957). *No and Yes*. New York: International Universities Press.
Stern, D. (1985). *The Interpersonal World of the Infant*. New York: Basic Books.
Stern, D., & the Boston Change Process Study Group (2004). Some implications of infant observations for psychoanalysis. In: A. Cooper (Ed.), *Contemporary Psychoanalysis in America: Leading Analysts Present Their Work*. Washington, DC: American Psychiatric Publishing, 2006, pp. 641–666.

Stern, D., Sander, L., Nahum, J., Harrison, A., Lyons-Ruth, K., Morgan, A., Bruschweilerstern, N., & Tronick, E. (1998). Non-interpretive mechanisms in psychoanalytic therapy: The "something more" than interpretation. *International Journal of Psychoanalysis*, 79: 903–921.

Trilling, L. (1964). *The Liberal Imagination*. London: Secker & Warburg.

Tsao, F., Liu, H., & Kuhl, P. (2006). Perception of native and non-native affricate-fricative contrasts: cross-language tests on adults and infants. *Journal of the Acoustical Society of America*, 120: 2285–2294.

Vitebsky, P. (2001). *The Shaman*. London: Duncan Baird.

Vygotsky, L. (1934). *Thought and Language*. Cambridge: MIT Press, 1962.

Vygotsky, L. (1962). Thought and word. In: P. Adams (Ed.), *Language in Thinking: Selected Readings*.London: Penguin Books, 1972, pp. 180–213.

Vygotsky, L. (1987). Thinking and speaking. In: R. Rieber & A. Carton (Eds.), *The Collected Papers of L. S. Vygotsky Vol. 1*. New York: Plenum, pp. 39–288.

Walter, M., & Fridman, E. (2004). *Shamanism: An Encyclopedia of World Beliefs, Practices and Cultures*. Santa Barbara, CA: ABC-CLIO.

Wan, M., Penketh, V., Salmon, M., & Abel, K. (2008). Content and style of speech from mothers with schizophrenia towards their infants. *Psychiatry Research*, 159: 109–114.

Werker, J., & Tees, R. (1984). Cross-language speech perception: Evidence for perceptual reorganization during the first year of life. *Infant Behavior and Development*, 7: 49–63.

Wilson, A., & Weinstein, L. (1992). Language and the psychoanalytic process: Psychoanalysis and Vygotskian psychology, Part II. *Journal of the American Psychoanalytic Association*, 40: 725–759.

Winnicott, D. W. (1965). Ego distortion in terms of true and false self. In: *The Maturational Process and the Facilitating Environment: Studies in the Theory of Emotional Development*. New York: International Universities Press, pp. 140–157.

Wittgenstein, L. (1922). *Tracticus Logico–Philosophicus*. London: Kegan Paul.

Index

aberrant language 6–8, 69–70, 151–152; characteristics 61–67; as idiographic data 78–79; and psychopathology 65 *see also* attachment, disturbed; clinical cases
Ainsworth, Mary 70
altered states of consciousness 37, 38, 43–44, 49, 66
animal intelligence 26, 31–32, 35
attachment: and culture 51; development of language and self 53–59; disturbed 69–76; infant-mother 10, 25–26, 33–34, 53–59, 151 *see also* motherese; separation-individuation
auditory system *see* hearing

belief systems 37–45; and culture 51; and primordial consciousness 38–41, 62 *see also* Trump, Donald
Beng culture 57
bicameral mind 15–17
bilingual model 53–59
Bowlby, John 53, 70

Chomsky, Noam 29–32
clinical cases: Caroline 7, 83–99; Charles 8, 111–118; Jacob 6–7, 7–8, 135–148; Jane 7, 101–109; Lisabeth 8–9, 119–133; and scientific method 77–79
concreteness 20, 23, 37, 50; in creativity 43, 44; and delusion/psychosis 39–40; symbolic equation 21, 22 *see also* primary process; primordial consciousness

consciousness 2, 16, 59; altered states of 37, 38, 43–44, 49, 66 *see also* primordial consciousness; reflective representational thought
creativity 43–45, 74
cults 39–40
culture(s): and primordial consciousness 38–39; self-centric/Western 13, 34, 39, 48, 56–57; socio-centric 32, 39, 44, 47–52, 57, 74

Darwin, Charles 25
delusions 39–40 *see also* belief systems; psychosis; primordial consciousness
Descartes, René 2, 11, 16, 31
differentiation 57, 58, 63; absence of 6, 17–18; and integration 6, 41; and pronoun use 74
disorganized attachment 70–71
dreaming/dreams: Freud on 6, 17–19, 23; as imagistic 26–27, 34; and primordial consciousness 25, 26–27, 41, 56; in tribal-spiritual cultures 48, 51 *see also* creativity
Dylan, Bob 43–45, 66, 74

Emde, R. 23
enactments 8, 35, 50, 51, 83, 149
Everett, Daniel 30, 32, 47, 49–51

fantasy, and phantasy 21–22
fetal development 25, 53–55, 70, 72
Fleck, Ludwik 38–39
fragmentation 6 *see also* integration

Freud, Sigmund: on dreaming 6, 17–19, 23; "Freudian slip" 38; and preconscious mind 19–20; reality principle 18; secondary process 11, 18 *see also* primary process, psychosis

grammar: development of 56; universal 29–32 *see also* Chomsky, Noam

hearing: deafness and sign language 55; *in utero* 25, 54–55

idiographic data 77–79
IDL (infant directed language) *see* motherese
imagistic mental activity 26–27, 149 *see also* dreaming/dreams
immediacy of experience principle 32, 49
implicit/procedural knowledge 22–23
integration, and differentiation 6, 41
introspection 2, 6, 11, 16, 57 *see also* recursion, reflective representational thought
Isaacs, Susan 20–21

Jaynes, Julian 15–17
Jung, C. G. 20

Klein, Melanie 17, 20, 21–22, 63, 65–66 *see also* paranoid-schizoid position; phantasy
Kuhl, Patricia 53

language 5–6, 9; bilingual mental processes of, 5; as hard-wired instinct, 30; as culturally determined 32; learning *in utero* and childhood 53–59, of primordial consciousness 65–67, of reflective representational thought 132, 150; relation to thought 33–35; second language development 55; as social development 33; speech development 56–58 *see also* aberrant language; separation-individuation
language instinct 30
linguistics, controversy within 29–32

Locke, John 40
logic, symmetric/asymmetric 22
Lyons-Ruth, K. 71

Main, Mary 70
maternal pathology 27, 69–71 *see also* attachment, disturbed
maternal vocalization *see* motherese
Matte-Blanco, I. 22
mirror systems 54
motherese 13–14, 26, 29–30, 54–55, 71 *see also* primordial consciousness
mother-infant bonding *see* attachment; motherese

neuroscience research, on attachment 53, 54, 71
nomothetic data 77

Palin, Sarah 62
paranoid-schizoid position 17, 20, 21, 65–66
patient essays *see* clinical cases
phantasy 17, 20–22
Pinker, Steven 14, 30, 32
Piraha 32, 49–52
political belief systems 40–41, 62
Prechtel, Martin 43, 44 *see also* creativity
preconscious mind 19–20, 21, 38 *see also* imagistic mental activity, symbolic equation
primary process 1–2, 17–18, 21–22, 23, 65–66 *see also* phantasy, symmetric/asymmetric logic, primordial consciousness
primordial consciousness 1, 6–7, 34–35; and belief systems 39–42, 48, 51, 62–63; characteristics 11–13, 74–75; and creativity 43–45; and culture 47–52; development in infancy 57–58; and dreaming 26–27, 56; in fetus 25, 53–55; and reflective representational thought 34–35, 37–38, 40
pronouns 6–7, 37–38, 50, 57, 58, 75, 150; disturbed use 71–72, 73, 74 *see also* aberrant language

projective identification 20–21, 63 *see also* paranoid-schizoid position, differentiation, primordial consciousness
prosody, infant-mother interaction 25, 54–55
psychopathology 12, 17, 20, 65–66, 69
psychosis 5–6, 39–40, 41–42, 65–66, 78 as social judgment 70, 72 *see also* aberrant language

recursion 11, 27, 29–32, 57 *see also* introspection, reflective representational thought; language
reductionism, neurobiological, in language theory 30
reflective representational thought: characteristics 11, 13, 31; development of 9, 55–59; and dreaming 18; and political belief 40–41; and primordial consciousness 34–35, 37–38, 40
religion *see* belief systems
REM sleep 25, 26, 53 *see also* primordial consciousness
representational thought, development of 22–23
Rizzuto, Anna-Marie 71–72, 75

schizophrenia 5–6, 15, 16
secure/insecure attachment 30, 70, 73, 74
Segal, Hannah 20, 21

self-centric cultures 13, 34, 39, 48, 56–57
separation-individuation 53, 56, 58, 72, 74, 151
shamanism 48–49
Shelton, Robert 44–45
socio-centric cultures 32, 39, 44, 47–52, 57, 74
speech, development of 56–58 *see also* aberrant language
splitting/dissociation 6 *see also* paranoid-schizoid position; projective identification
symbolic equation 21, 22 *see also* imagistic mental activity, preconscious mind
symbolism 22, 27 *see also* reflective representational thought
symmetric/asymmetric logic 22

thought, relation to language 33–35
transformational grammar 30–31
tribal/spiritual cultures 32, 43, 49–52
Trump, Donald 38, 62–67, 72–74

undifferentiation *see* differentiation; primordial consciousness
universal grammar 29–32 *see also* recursion; language instinct

Vygotsky, Lev 33

Western/self-centric cultures 13, 34, 48, 56–57

Lightning Source UK Ltd.
Milton Keynes UK
UKHW021535140520
363247UK00006B/51